LOVED

Loved

Learning to Rest

Clara Jones

LOVED: LEARNING TO REST
The Summit Church
6600 Crystal Hill Road
North Little Rock, Arkansas 72118
TheSummitChurch.org

Unless otherwise noted, Scripture quotations are from THE HOLY BIBLE, NEW INTERNATIONAL VERSION® NIV®. Copyright © 1973, 1978, 1984 by International Bible Society®. Used by permission. All rights reserved worldwide.

Scripture quotations marked "Phillips" are taken from The New Testament in Modern English, copyright © 1958, 1959, 1960 J.B. Phillips and 1947, 1952, 1955, 1957 The Macmillan Company, New York. Used by permission. All rights reserved.

Scripture quotations identified "KJV" are from the *King James Version*.

Scripture quotations marked "NKJV" are taken from the New King James Version®. Copyright © 1982 by Thomas Nelson, Inc. Used by permission. All rights reserved.

Scripture quotations marked "CEB" are taken from the Common English Bible®, CEB® Copyright © 2010, 2011 by Common English Bible.™ Used by permission. All rights reserved worldwide. The "CEB" and "Common English Bible" trademarks are registered in the United States Patent and Trademark Office by Common English Bible. Use of either trademark requires the permission of Common English Bible.

ISBN: 1519739826
ISBN 13: 9781519739827

© 2015 Clara Jones

All rights reserved. No part of this publication may be reproduced or transmitted in any form or by any means, electronic or mechanical, including photocopy, recording, or any information storage and retrieval system, without permission in writing from the publisher. Requests for permission to make copies of any part of this publication should be sent to: info@thesummitchurch.org.

Editor: Tim Grissom

Printed in the United States of America

19 18 17 16 15   1 2 3 4 5

*There is a place of quiet rest,
Near to the heart of God,
A place where sin cannot molest,
Near to the heart of God.*

*Oh, Jesus, blest Redeemer,
Sent from the heart of God,
Hold us, who wait before thee,
Near to the heart of God!*

—Cleland B. McAfee

Contents

Introduction ··· xi
Suggestions for Using This Study ······································ xiii

His First Wooing: Desiring All of Me ···································· 1

Lesson 1   The Battle ·· 3
Lesson 2   The Victory ·· 15

His Second Wooing: Calling Me His Princess ························· 25

Lesson 3   The Confrontation of a Stronghold ························· 27
Lesson 4   The Strength in Trusting ······································ 39
Lesson 5   The Power of God's Word ····································· 49

His Third Wooing: Lavishing His Grace on Me ······················· 59

Lesson 6   Awakened to Grace ··· 61
Lesson 7   Enlightened to God's Great Power ·························· 71
Lesson 8   Rooted and Grounded in Love ······························· 87

His Continual Wooing: Always Waiting with Open Arms ··········· 95

Lesson 9   Running to Christ ··· 97

Going Deeper ·· 109
Leader's Guide ··· 209

Dear sister in Christ,

"I pray that you, being rooted and established in love, may have power, together with all the saints, to grasp how wide and long and high and deep is the love of Christ, and to know this love that surpasses knowledge—that you may be filled to the measure of all the fullness of God" (Ephesians 3:17-19).

With much love for you because of Christ's passionate love for me,
Clara

Introduction

This is not the usual Bible study; it's really a love story. It's the story of Christ's stubborn pursuit of me—to convince me of His incomprehensible love and of His passionate desire to have all of my love and devotion.

Christ pursued me even when I spurned Him, continuing on in my pride, selfish ambitions, and love of self. He saw deep into my soul and had compassion because He knew that what I was longing for, only He could give—and He desperately wanted to give it to me. That *it*, I learned, was Christ Himself.

Knowing Christ and His great love has a transforming power. It has radically changed me from being an insecure, self-confident (yes, you can be both), heavily burdened Christian into a secure, Christ-confident, set free, passionate lover of Christ.

I felt compelled to write this story in a Bible study format because I know that Christ is pursuing you, too, with the same intense passion with which He pursued and continues to pursue me. Christ said, "But I, when I am lifted up from the earth, will draw all men to myself" (John 12:32). He is longing for you to stop striving and flailing and to find rest in His arms. My prayer is that, as I tell my story and you study the passages from the Bible that God used to speak to me, you too will fall in love with your Savior and find rest for your soul.

. . .

I was brought up in a wonderful Christian home with a father and mother who loved me and loved their Savior. We not only went to church faithfully but my parents also consistently had family devotions with my twelve siblings and me and taught us the Word of God. My dad was a bivocational pastor and spent much time studying the Bible and reading Christian books. He loved the Word of God and taught me to love it too. At a young age I became convinced that the "word of God is quick, and powerful, and sharper than any twoedged sword, piercing even to the dividing asunder of soul and spirit, and of the joints and marrow, and is a discerner of the thoughts and intents of the heart" (Hebrews 4:12 KJV). My parents had us memorize verses on a regular basis and even used scripture memorization (sometimes an entire book of the Bible) as an occasional means of discipline when we fought with one another.

I accepted Christ as my Savior from the penalty of sin at the age of four or five at an evangelistic meeting at our church. Even as a young child, I understood that I could not do anything to receive eternal salvation from sin's penalty, but I did not understand how I needed Christ to save me from sin itself on a daily basis or how I needed to cling to Him alone for that salvation. I thought that the Christian life was about my serving God and doing what He expected of me so that I would be pleasing to Him.

For years I confessed my sins over and over but never was able to come to the point of freedom, joy, and peace because not long after I confessed and felt a sense of relief, I would sin again and once again would be faced with defeat and feelings of failure. I basically lived under the weight of condemnation. I poured out my heart to God and longed for victory and freedom but was constantly evaluating myself, and when I looked inward, all I found was a sinful person.

The Christian life was not liberating to me. It was burdensome. I didn't understand scriptures like 1 John 5:3, which says that "his commands are not burdensome." I could better relate to the words of Romans 7:24, "What a wretched man I am! Who will rescue me from this body of death?" I didn't understand Paul's answer in verse 25: "Thanks be to God—through Jesus Christ our Lord!" Nor did I understand what it meant that "there is no condemnation for those who are in Christ Jesus, because through Christ Jesus the law of the Spirit of life set me free from the law of sin and death" (Romans 8:1).

I interpreted verses that spoke of iniquity in my heart (Psalm 66:18) and confession of sin (1 John 1:9) to mean that God would not listen to me if I had unconfessed sin in my life. And I knew that I dealt with sin constantly. I tried to live my life to glorify God, but I felt I could never satisfy God's expectations of me. He demanded that I be holy as He is holy (1 Peter 1:16), and consequently, I thought that it was my job to make myself holy.

I don't know how much of this you can relate to personally, but I wanted to share this background with you because I believe there are many Christians who know a lot in their heads that has never truly reached their hearts. We say we are trusting Christ to live the Christian life and may believe we really are, but in reality we are striving to do it on our own. This Bible study homes in on those lessons that God taught me over a span of ten years, which revealed to me the roots of my sins and how I could be set free. It is also a story of how I fell deeply in love with the One who set me free from the burden of sin that I carried for so long.

Suggestions for Using This Study

This study consists of nine lessons followed by a section for more in-depth study of Scripture called "Going Deeper." The nine lessons tell my story and provide the foundational truths God revealed to me that taught me to rest in His love. "Going Deeper" provides an opportunity to pore over these biblical truths introduced in the nine lessons, and because God's Word was so powerful in transforming my own life, I strongly suggest that you make time to complete it. A suggested schedule for "Going Deeper" is given at the end of each week's lesson.

This study can be completed independently or in conjunction with teaching DVDs and small group discussion.

In the writing of this study, I primarily used the New International Version of the Bible. To avoid confusion when filling in the blanks, you will want to use the New International Version.

His First Wooing

Desiring All of Me

**I belong to my lover,
and his desire is for me.**

Song of Songs 7:10

One

The Battle

Frustration Over the Losing Battle

The pattern of being defeated by sin intensified when I began to have children. Motherhood revealed a sin problem I didn't know I had: anger. For years I tried to be patient and kind with the eight children God had blessed me with, but it seemed they were continually doing things that sparked my temper. After twelve or thirteen years of this battle, I did a personal Bible study on child rearing and anger—mainly from the book of Proverbs. I wanted to learn how God really felt about anger. I knew that He got angry at times, and consequently, I would justify my lashing out at my kids. But in doing that study, I came to the conclusion that disciplining my children in anger was both sinful and counterproductive. I also realized that I was what Proverbs describes as a "foolish woman" because of my inability to control my temper (Proverbs 12:16; 29:8, 11). I knew that if I could not get victory over my anger, I would be in danger of "tearing my house down with my own hands" (see Proverbs 14:1). There were other sins in my life, but this sin of uncontrollable anger was the one that bothered me the most. I dearly loved my children and knew that I was hurting them with my anger; but when they put me to the test, I could not help but get angry.

I came to the conclusion that I had to get control over my temper, so I began to pray regularly for the fruit of the Spirit. However, as much as I was determined to get rid of anger and to be full of love, joy, and peace, I still could not get victory.

This intense desire for victory, but experience of defeat, frustrated me to the point of despair. I just wanted to die and go to heaven so I wouldn't have to deal with my sin any longer. I wasn't suicidal but just wished I could go on to heaven because I thought I could never change as long as I was on this earth. My constant thought was, *Why do I not have peace and joy like a Christian should?*

I know now that God had to bring me to this point of desperation before He could begin to set me free. Otherwise, I would think that victory over sin was something I had accomplished in my own strength.

Making It Personal

1. Are you desperate to change? Yes / No

Is there sin (or sins) that you deal with on a regular basis? Yes / No

What are the sins that you struggle to get victory over? _____

_____

2. You probably wouldn't be doing this Bible study if you didn't desire victory over these sins, but are you *desperate* to change? Read Romans 7:14-24. Do you relate to Paul's struggle with sin? Yes / No

What did Paul say in this passage that describes your own struggle with sin?

_____

_____

_____

_____

Can you relate to Paul's desperation to be set free? Yes / No

Do you hate your sin to the point that you are willing to do anything God tells you in order to overcome it? Yes / No

Read Romans 7:24-25. There is hope for you to be set free from sin, but you must first come to the point of understanding that you desperately need a Savior—not only from the penalty of sin (hell) but also from sin itself on a daily basis.

Realization of My Incapability

The continual frustration I experienced drove me to the realization that I was completely incapable of producing the fruit of the Spirit. Around this time, a friend from church told me about an unbeliever saying to her, "Christians need God because they are weak people." I started to think about what I would have said to the unbeliever to defend Christians, but then my friend said, "You know she is right. She is absolutely right." And that was exactly what I needed to hear at that moment. I realized that I had to get to the point of feeling completely powerless before I would accept God's help.

Making It Personal

1. Are you okay with your weakness? Yes / No

2. Although this may sound counterintuitive in our think-positive culture, we need to accept our own weakness. Read 2 Corinthians 12:7-9. What does verse 9 teach us about weakness?
   _____

Our weakness causes us to see our need for God and keeps us dependent on Him. Then *His strength does for us what we are powerless to do for ourselves.*

Like a drowning person fighting to stay above water, I had to stop trying to save myself and allow my Life Saver to come rescue me. At this point, however, I still could not be rescued. I did not realize I was entirely helpless to save myself and was not completely clinging to the One who could rescue me. I longed for God to fill me with His Spirit, but I didn't realize that there were some deeper issues that were producing the anger.

Attempting to Serve Two Masters

Around this time I went to a conference in the Czech Republic (my husband and I were missionaries in Slovakia at the time) where the theme was "The Role of the Holy Spirit in a Movement of God."* When I found out what the theme would be, I was very excited because I anticipated that God would answer my prayer about how to be filled with the Spirit and experience His fruit. As we studied about the work

---

* This conference turned out to be a key event. I will simply refer to it as "the conference" in the first three lessons.

of the Holy Spirit, there were some key things taught from God's Word that really caused me to see the root of my problem. We were asked to write down the "lines" (essentially, the rationalizations, doubts, and accusations) our sinful nature tells us that cause us to not do "the good we want to do" (Romans 7:18-19). I wrote:

What will people think?
I don't have time.
You're wasting your talents.
You're not capable of responding right.
Are people noticing?

This exercise was helpful to me because God began showing me from the things I wrote down the roots of my sin: motivations of pride and selfishness. The first line I had written down ("What will people think?") revealed a major problem: I was trying to please God and people at the same time, and I couldn't consistently do it. For example, it was not unusual for me to get angry at home when we were expecting guests and the children were not doing what I had told them to do about cleaning the house. I would get angry at them because if my house was not clean and in order when people came, it reflected negatively on me and my housekeeping. I could not be controlled by the Spirit of God because fear of man was in the way. God had been working in my heart about this very issue sometime earlier as I had been reading Galatians 1:10: "Am I now trying to win the approval of men, or of God? Or am I trying to please men? If I were still trying to please men, I would not be a servant of Christ." God also used Matthew 6:24 where Jesus said, "No one can serve two masters," to show me that I was trying to serve two masters by trying to please both God and people. However, now I was not only convicted, but I also began to see what I needed to do about it. I fell on my knees and surrendered to God and told Him I would serve Him and Him alone. I would do whatever He wanted me to do in order not to be so concerned about what people thought about me.

I began to see how fear of man permeated almost everything I did. I wanted people to think we were good parents so I would get angry when the children were disobedient in the presence of others. I wanted people to think I was intelligent, so when I would speak in Slovak, I wanted to speak perfectly in order to impress people with my ability. It was important to me that people thought I had a beautiful singing voice and that I looked pretty. I felt insecure at times when talking with people because I was concerned about what they would think of me. I was fearful to tell people about Christ for fear they would reject me. Though I wanted God to be glorified in the things I did and said, I knew that as long as I was seeking recognition or living to please myself, God was not being glorified.

Making It Personal

1. What "lines" does your sinful nature give you? Ask God to bring them to your mind, and as you think of them, write them here:

   _____

   _____

   _____

   _____

   _____

Before going further, stop and ask God to speak to you and reveal to you, through the things you wrote down and through His Word, the root causes of the sin(s) that you deal with. Ask Him to purge these sins from your life and set you free. He is your only hope for being set free from serving sin.

2. Now let's look at some root causes that could be the motivation behind the sin in your life. Read Galatians 1:10. According to this verse, what can keep us from being a servant of Christ?
   _____

Can you relate to this root sin? Yes / No

In what ways is this root sin affecting you?

_____

_____

_____

3. Read Matthew 6:19-33 and 1 Timothy 6:6-11. What is it that Jesus says keeps us from serving God (Matthew 6:24) and that Paul says is a root of all kinds of evil (1 Timothy 6:10?
   _____

Do you struggle with this root sin? Yes / No
If so, describe your struggle. _____

_____

_____

_____

4. Read 2 Timothy 4:10. What kept Demas from wanting to stay with Paul (who was expending his life serving God)?
   _____

5. Read 1 John 2:15-17. These verses teach that we cannot love the things of this world and love God at the same time. Do you see some indications in your life that you are seeking to find fulfillment in what this world has to offer rather than in God? Yes / No
What are they? _____

_____

_____

These are only some of the heart issues at the root of more visible sins. For a more thorough list, read Galatians 5:17-21. Which of these sins can you relate to? _____

_____

_____

_____

6. You may say, *But I have already surrendered my life to God.* I, too, thought I had surrendered my life to God. I had even gone overseas as a missionary! But God was making clear to me

that I had an idol—something I valued as highly, or more highly, than I valued Him—in the form of the praise of men. As my pastor Bill Elliff has said, "Whatever I look to and think I have to have in order to have a meaningful life becomes my idol, and it will control and dominate my life and ultimately destroy me."

Think about Bill's statement. God sees loving the praise of men, loving money, and loving the world as idols. Besides those already mentioned, can you see any other idols in your life that are competing with your love for God? Yes / No

If so, what are they? _____

_____

_____

Spend some time talking to God about your idols. Be honest with Him. Do you still want them in your life, or are you ready to forsake them and make Him alone your first and greatest love? If you are not at the place where you can surrender your life completely to Him, it is probably because you do not really know His heart. You cannot surrender to someone you do not trust. You cannot fully trust someone you do not know. If you feel you cannot trust Him, will you commit yourself to really getting to know Him through His Word?

> O, taste and see that the Lord is good: blessed is the man that trusteth in Him. (Psalm 34:8 KJV)

No Makeup for a Week

Following the conference, I became exceedingly wary of doing or saying things for the approval of others. One of the things I felt God wanted me to do in order to be set free from the fear of man was to stop wearing makeup for a while. This seemed to me to be a drastic measure. I had a very difficult time allowing people to see me without makeup, but after the conference, I went without makeup for a week. I wanted very much to not care what people thought of me. At first, I felt truly free. I now had no one to please but God, and I found such joy and peace. However, after a week, going without makeup became enslaving also. There was no freedom in that. The Christian life is not about keeping rules and regulations, but about freedom in Christ—which we will get to later.

I was trying to change a heart attitude by making outward adjustments. What I really needed was for God to meet the need of my heart. At this point, I did not understand that I needed *God* completely for this heart change. I thought since the problem was with me, I needed to change myself. My big mistake was looking to self to do what only God can do.

Song for Worship and Meditation: "Weak Man" sung and written by Leeland, from the album *Love Is On the Move*, 2009

Memory Verse

Taste and see that the LORD is good; blessed is the man who takes refuge in him. Fear the LORD, you his saints, for those who fear him lack nothing. (Psalm 34:8-9)

Going Deeper

Suggested Daily Schedule for Week 1

Day 1   Complete Lesson 1.

Day 2   Read Romans 6; complete pages 111-114.

Day 3   Read Romans 7; complete pages 115-116.

Day 4   Read Romans 8:1-16; complete pages 117-119.

Day 5   Read 2 Corinthians 12:1-10; Matthew 9:10-13; Luke 14:15-24; 2 Corinthians 10:12, 17- 18; 1 Corinthians 1:17-31; complete pages 120-122.

Viewer Guide
Session 1: Understanding Our Weakness

We will never live in victory over sin as long as we think that having victory has anything to do with _____.

Romans 7:18-21 describes our complete helplessness to do anything _____.

Jeremiah 17:9 (NIV) says that our hearts are _____ _____ _____ _____, desperately _____ and _____ _____.

Galatians 5:17, 19-21 teaches us that because we all have a _____ _____, we cannot do not the good we want to do.

Isaiah 64:6 says that "_____ of us have become like one who is unclean," and even our righteous acts are like _____ _____ in God's sight."

John 15:4-5
Jesus also talked about our weakness. In verse 4 He said we must _____ ____ _____ in order to bear fruit. In verse 5 He said that apart from Him we can do _____. If we don't abide in Him, we will not bear _____ fruit. We are like branches that are good for _____. But if we remain in Him, and He in us, we will bear _____ _____.

We will never be able to take hold of the power of God to save us from any sin we are dealing with until we realize that _____ is our only hope.

Is God upset with us because we are drawn to sin even though we know that we have been saved from it?

Psalm 103:1-18
The Lord crowns us with _____ and _____ (v. 4).

The Lord is _____, _____, _____ ___ _____, and _____ __ _____ (v. 8).

He does not treat us _____ _____ _____ _____ or repay us what we deserve for our sins.

His love for those who fear Him is as great as the _____ _____ _____ _____ _____ _____.

He understands our _____. He knows that we are _____. The Lord's love is with those who fear Him _____ _____ ____ _____.
This means He has _____ _____ ____ and He _____ _____.

So, according to this passage, is God upset with us because we are drawn to sin even though we know that we have been saved from it?

The answer is ____. God understands our _____.

Romans 5:6-10
If God had compassion on us and saved us when we were completely helpless and separated from Him in our sin, how much more will He have compassion on us ____ _____ _____ _____ _____ still _____ _____ apart from Him to do anything good!
We should be okay with our weakness because we have a Savior who is _____.
Romans 7:21-8:4
Verse 25 says that _____ has rescued us through Jesus Christ our Lord. _____ has already won the victory for us!

Romans 8:1 says there is no _____ for us.
What did He do about our sin according to Romans 8:4?
He sent His Son to _____ ____ _____ _____ _____ _____ to the sinful nature.
God understands that we are incapable, even as Christians, of doing anything good. He understands our _____.

Becoming aware of the _____ _____ _____ _____ ____ _____ and of our continual need for _____ ____ _____ ____ causes us to fall in love with our Savior.

Two

The Victory

A Mind Set on What the Spirit Desires

I learned a second lesson at the conference we attended in the Czech Republic: I desperately needed the Spirit of God to take over my mind and control my thinking. Romans 8:5 addresses this when it says, "Those who live according to the sinful nature have their minds set on what that nature desires; but those who live in accordance with the Spirit have their minds set on what the Spirit desires."

Several months prior to the conference while reading Romans 8, I had had the thought: *This is the answer to being controlled by the Spirit. I must keep my mind "set on what the Spirit desires."* However, because I was not then fully surrendered to what He desired, it was difficult for me to know what it was that He wanted me to do in a given situation. But after the experience at the conference of surrendering to God to serve Him and Him alone, I began to try to do what I thought this verse was saying I needed to do in order to be controlled by the Spirit of God.

In the days following, whenever I began to get angry or to have thoughts of wanting people to admire me, or when I would feel selfish and not want to be a servant to my family or deal with my children's misconduct, I would ask myself, *What does the Spirit want me to do at this moment?* And then I would surrender to whatever that was. In that way I tried to "set my mind on what the Spirit desires." As I put this into practice, God would often reveal to me what the real issues were when I found myself getting angry at the kids. For example, if I had guests coming and the children were not cooperating, I could be at peace in dealing with them because I realized that it was more important to God that I dealt with my children in love than that I had my house in showcase order.

This practice of setting my mind on what the Spirit desires made a difference in my life. At the time, I thought that surrendering my desires to the Spirit's desires was the answer to getting victory over my sinful nature. I was beginning to realize the need to look to God for change instead of trying to change myself, and when I began to ask God that I might see things from His perspective and know what He desired for me, He began to show me. The truth is, however, that when I began attempting to set my mind on what the Spirit desires, I began to experience victory over sin, not because I had discovered a formula that worked, but because I was beginning to trust God enough to surrender every thought "to make it obedient to Christ" (2 Corinthians 10:5).

It was not until much later that I understood that I actually had Romans 8:5 backward. I did not need to *do* anything to be filled with the Spirit of God. Notice that this verse says that "those who live in accordance with the Spirit *have* their minds set on what the Spirit desires." It does not say that we need to set our minds on what the Spirit desires *in order* to live in accordance with the Spirit. Living in accordance with the Spirit actually *causes* our minds to be set on what the Spirit desires. You see, I was trying to find what I needed to *do* to be controlled by the Spirit of God when what I really needed was to be transformed by a renewal of my thinking about who God is, how He viewed me, and what Christ had already accomplished on my behalf. (This renewal of my thinking was a process that was to come later.)

Making It Personal

1. Read Romans 8:1-15. If you do not have the Spirit of Christ, what does that mean about you (v. 9)? _____

What happens if the Spirit of God lives in you (v. 9)? _____
_____

What do you think this verse means when it says that we are "controlled by the Spirit"? _____
_____

For a clearer understanding of what this phrase means, read verse 9 in the New King James Version:

> But you are not in the flesh but in the Spirit, if indeed the Spirit of God dwells in you. Now if anyone does not have the Spirit of Christ, he is not His.

Being "controlled by the Spirit" means that the sinful nature is no longer our master.

2. Satan wants us to think that we are still slaves to the sinful nature, but we are not. We now live in the realm of the Spirit, and the Spirit now has control over us in the same way that an earthly king has rule over the subjects of his realm. Read Romans 6:1-7. What happened to the sinful nature of each one who has been (spiritually) baptized into Christ's death (v. 6)?

_____

3. Read Romans 6:8-14 and fill in the missing words.

Verse 11: Count yourselves _____ to sin but _____ to God in Christ Jesus.

Verse 13: Do not _____ the parts of your body to sin . . . but rather _____ yourselves to God, as those who have been brought from death to life; and _____ the parts of your body to him as instruments of righteousness.

4. What situations do you find yourself in where you most often fall into sin?

_____
_____

When you are in these situations, what is the Spirit's desire for you? What does God want you to do in these situations?

_____
_____
_____

Asking myself these questions helped me in transferring my allegiance to my new Master. I believed at the time that the key to victory over sin was *surrender*. It is true that if you are not surrendered to God, it will be difficult for you to even know what He wants you to do in a given situation. However, the deeper issue is trust because we cannot surrender ourselves in obedience to someone we cannot trust.

Are you able to trust Him enough to offer the parts of your body right now as instruments of righteousness to Him in the situations that you wrote down? _____ If so, will you take time to tell Him so now? If not, will you ask Him to teach you about Himself so that you can learn to trust Him?

5. Read 2 Corinthians 10:4-5. How do we "demolish arguments and every pretension that sets itself up against the knowledge of God"? _____
_____

Notice that it is the knowledge of God that is to be our goal. When we reject the wrong thoughts about who God is and replace them with the truth of who He is, we find that we can trust Him and gladly offer our bodies as instruments of righteousness to Him.

The Beginning of a Heart Change

I began to see a difference in my life. Whereas I had constantly seemed to be defeated in the past, the Spirit began to take over and change my self-centered thoughts to Christ-centered thoughts, giving me the power to do what God desired. I can still remember the first time one of my children was yelling because he was angry about something, and I felt complete peace. God was doing for me what I had not been able to do for myself. In the months that followed, I experienced victory like I never had before. I especially saw a difference in dealing with my children. Once I recognized the root of my actions, the Spirit of God stopped the sinful, self-centered thoughts in my mind where they began and before I acted on them.

It was as if I had been looking away from God, but He took my face in His hands and said, "Clara, look here. Look at Me." I was beginning to learn that

> what the law was powerless to do in that it was weakened by the sinful nature, God did by sending his own Son in the likeness of sinful man to be a sin offering. And so he condemned sin in sinful man, in order that the righteous requirements of the law might be fully met in us, who do not live according to the sinful nature but according to the Spirit. (Romans 8:3-4)

I began to understand that I must get my eyes off myself and others and onto Christ.

Revelation of the Need to Pursue God and Not Victory

For a long time, I had prayed for the fruit of the Spirit to be manifested in my life. God finally showed me that the fruit of the Spirit is not something I can work up. The fruit was not what I should have been seeking. I needed to be seeking Christ Himself, and as Christ became my focus, the Spirit of Christ began to produce in me what I could never do for myself. I began to realize that without even trying, I had love, joy, peace, patience, kindness, goodness, faithfulness, gentleness, and self-control as I was focused on Him and filled with Him. I was beginning to realize that being filled with the Spirit was not following a formula but knowing and being filled with a Person. But I still had much to learn. I was just beginning to really *know* Him.

Making It Personal

1. What is your primary focus in your Christian life? Are you focused on pleasing God and getting victory over sin, or are you focused on Christ and knowing Him? _____
   _____

2. Read Philippians 3:7-14. What did Paul want more than anything else? _____
   _____
   _____

Paul pressed hard after the goal of knowing _____ (v. 10), which is why Christ laid hold of Paul—that he might know Christ. I believe the prize for Paul (mentioned in v. 14) was Christ Himself, as Paul indicates in verses 8-10 and verse 20.

3. Read Hebrews 12:1-2. On whom are we to fix our eyes? _____.

I believe that *we* were the joy that was set before Christ (Luke 15:3-7). He rejoices over every sinner who repents. What is the desire of the Lover of our souls according to Song of Songs 7:10? His desire is for _____! He wants us to repent of our sins because He desires to have our unadulterated love. He longs for our complete devotion because he wants to have intimacy with us. Oh, what a wonderful Savior!

Song for Worship and Meditation: "I Will Lift My Eyes," sung and written by Bebo Norman, from the album *Between the Dreaming and the Coming True*, 2006

Memory Verse

For what the law was powerless to do in that it was weakened by the sinful nature, God did by sending his own Son in the likeness of sinful man to be a sin offering. And so he condemned sin in sinful man, in order that the righteous requirements of the law might be fully met in us, who do not live according to the sinful nature but according to the Spirit. (Romans 8:3-4)

Going Deeper

Suggested Daily Schedule for Week 2

Day 1   Complete Lesson 2.

Day 2   Read Romans 12:1-2; Ephesians 4:22-24; Colossians 3:9-10; Romans 13:12-14; complete pages 123-125.

Day 3   Read Galatians 5:16-26; complete pages 126-127.

Day 4   Read John 7:37-39; 1 Corinthians 12:12-13; Ephesians 5:18-21; Colossians 3:14-18; complete pages 128-129.

Day 5   Read Philippians 3; complete pages 130-133.

Viewer Guide
Session 2: Christ Really Is the Answer

John 5:39-40
Jesus said the truth of God's Word that is able to save us is the truth we find in _____ Himself.

Colossians 2:1-3
Paul says he is struggling for the Colossians "so that they may have the full riches of complete understanding, in order that they may know the mystery of God, namely _____."

The Colossians whom Paul was writing to were _____ (see Colossians 1:2, 2:6).
This means that we can be believers in Christ and still not completely understand _____ _____ and what He has done for us.

Verses 4-5
Paul did not want anyone to "_____ _____ by _____ _____."

Paul was delighted to see how _____ _____ _____ ____ _____ was.

Verses 6-7
Paul instructed the Colossians to continue to live in Christ in the same way that they had _____ _____.

According to Galatians 3:2-3, we received Christ ____ _____.

If we are to continue to live in Christ the same way that we received Him, then the way we are to continue to live in Him as Christians is ____ _____.

According to verse 7, we are to be rooted and built up in _____.

Being built up in Christ _____ our faith, and the result is _____.

Verse 8
The way we avoid false doctrine and legalism is by _____ ____ _____.

Verses 9-10
We are made complete ____ _____.

Verses 11-12
We have been set apart as the people of God by our hearts being "circumcised" (Romans 2:28-29; Philippians 3:3). _____ has done the work of putting off the sinful nature and making our hearts clean (v. 11)? "____ _____ you were also circumcised, in the putting off of the sinful nature, not with a circumcision done by the hands of men but with the circumcision _____ ____ _____."

Verses 13-15
According to verse 13, we were able to do _____ to make ourselves righteous. We were _____!

_____ raised us from the dead _____ _____.

Verses 16-17
According to verse 17, the observances of the law were abolished. The reality (or fulfillment) of these observances is found ____ _____.

Verses 18-19
If someone is trying to make you believe that the Christian life is about your doing certain things in order to keep God pleased with you, that person has lost connection with _____ _____, who is _____ (v. 19).

Verses 20-23
There is ____ value in trying to beat our bodies into submission to God by adhering to rules. We are _____ to restrain our sinful natures by keeping laws. Verse 23 says, "Such regulations . . . _____ _____ _____ in restraining sensual indulgence."

Obtaining victory over the sin in our lives rests entirely on _____.
No matter what the need of your heart is, _____ really is the answer.

His Second Wooing

Calling Me His Princess

Listen, O daughter, consider and give ear:
Forget your people and your father's house.
The king is enthralled by your beauty;
honor him, for he is your lord.

Psalm 45:10-11

Three

The Confrontation of a Stronghold

The Fruit of Insecurity

Two other issues I had struggled with my entire life were insecurity and pride. It may seem ironic that I struggled with these at the same time, but I really think the two are just opposite sides of the same coin. From the time I was young, I found self-worth in my abilities. Consequently, I felt proud when people noticed the things I excelled in but felt insecure when I could not do something well or when people failed to see what I had achieved. I craved approval and praise for my accomplishments.

I remember being taught in the Christian high school I attended how to find self-worth in who we are as God's children. However, the way it was presented was that people with low self-esteem needed to realize how much God valued them as His children. I couldn't relate to that. I didn't think I had low self-esteem. If anything, I thought too highly of myself. I didn't think I had a problem believing God loved and accepted me. It was the approval of people that I longed for.

For years I lived in this bondage to perform, not knowing how to be set free. I tried to do things for the glory of God and not care what people thought of me, but my efforts were in vain. Thankfully, at the same time that God set me free from anger, I began to see that some of the same roots that caused me to deal with anger also incited my insecurity and pride.

Though I had repented of trying to have two masters and began to make a practice of "setting my mind on what the Spirit desires" (Romans 8:5), I realized in the months and years following the conference that I continued to battle with caring what people thought about me. It was an especially intense battle whenever we would go to our missionary conferences—both because we were with peers, who were doing the same type of ministry that we were doing, and also because they only knew me from a distance. Because I had always found my self-worth in my abilities, I would feel very insecure at these conferences because people did not know what my gifts or accomplishments were. I found that I would really struggle for recognition because I felt that if they did not know my giftedness, spirituality, or wisdom, they would not value me as a person or as a missionary. I really longed for their friendship, but I had always felt that the reason people wanted to be friends with me was because of my gifts and abilities, and knowing that these peers were unaware of these things left me feeling insecure.

About three years after the conference on the work of the Holy Spirit, we again went to the Czech Republic for our bi-annual missionary conference.* As usual, I began to have deep feelings of insecurity. I prayed (as I had gotten into a habit of doing) that the Lord would help me live for Him and Him alone and give me victory, but these feelings of insecurity would not go away. I was frustrated that although I had thought God had taken away my concern of what others thought of me, I continued to battle with it.

At the conference, Dave Patty spoke on repentance. He said that because repentance is a change of mind, it brings about complete change, and we will not fall into the same sins that we were committing before we repented. As I listened to him, I began to wonder if I had ever truly repented of serving two masters because I still did not have victory over longing for the recognition of people. That afternoon I had some time alone, so I spent the time reading my Bible and asking God to show me why I still found myself in this battle. I searched God's Word for verses that talk about how we can be free from sin and, more specifically, how I could get victory over bringing glory to myself that belongs to God.

Making It Personal

The following verses spoke to me that day. Read them for yourself and answer the questions.

> It is for freedom that Christ has set us free. Stand firm, then, and do not let yourselves be burdened again by a yoke† of slavery. (Galatians 5:1)

1. Do you feel burdened by a yoke of slavery? Yes / No

2. What yoke of slavery are you carrying? _____
_____
_____

> You, my brothers, were called to be free. But do not use your freedom to indulge the sinful nature; rather, serve one another in love. The entire law is summed up in a single command: "Love your neighbor as yourself." (Galatians 5:13-14)

---

* This second conference turned out to be another key event. I will simply refer to it as "the conference" throughout the rest of this study.

† A yoke was a wooden bar used to join a pair of working oxen so that they could pull a load together.

3. Do you find it difficult to love others as you love yourself? Yes / No

> I now find that when I am basking in God's love for me, I cannot help but love people. Loving people is a natural result of being filled with the Spirit because the Spirit cannot help but love people!

> We do not dare to classify or compare ourselves with some who commend themselves. When they measure themselves by themselves and compare themselves with themselves, they are not wise. (2 Corinthians 10:12)

4. Do you have a habit of measuring yourself by comparing yourself with others? Yes / No

5. How does this make you feel about yourself? _____
_____

6. How does this make you feel about others? _____
_____

> But, "Let him who boasts boast in the Lord." For it is not the one who commends himself who is approved, but the one whom the Lord commends. (2 Corinthians 10:17-18)

7. Does praise for your Savior naturally flow from your lips, or are you prone to talk more about yourself? _____

> If I must boast, I will boast of the things that show my weakness. (2 Corinthians 11:30)

> But [the Lord] said to me, "My grace is sufficient for you, for my power is made perfect in weakness." Therefore I will boast all the more gladly about my weaknesses, so that Christ's power may rest on me." (2 Corinthians 12:9)

8. In what ways has God used your weakness (neediness) in order to show His power through your life? _____
_____
_____

In Galatians 5, just before the fruit of the Spirit is listed, the acts of the sinful nature are listed. Read verses 19-21 and see if you can identify any of these acts in your own life.

9. What, if any, acts of the sinful nature were you able to identify in your life? _____
_____
_____

10. Now read verses 22-25. Which list more describes you, the one in verses 19-21 or the one in verses 22-23? _____

Spend some time in prayer, pouring your heart out to God. If you are ready to be set free from your slavery to sin, tell Him so. Surrender the control of your life to Him, allowing Him to fill you with His Spirit. Before you pray, consider these words of Jesus:

> Which of you fathers, if your son asks for a fish, will give him a snake instead? Or if he asks for an egg, will give him a scorpion? If you then, though you are evil, know how to give good gifts to your children, how much more will your Father in heaven give the Holy Spirit to those who ask him! (Luke 11:11-13)

The Root of Insecurity

As I read the list of sins in Galatians 5:19-21, God directed my attention to the words "selfish ambition." I immediately knew that this was the sin that I was battling with. It was the root of my insecurities. I found many verses that convicted me about selfish ambition, but I could not find an answer to why I could not get victory over this.

That evening at supper my husband, Danny, and I "happened" to sit with the speaker, Dave Patty, and his wife, Connie. I began to pour out my soul in hopes of getting some clarity over this issue. Dave assured me that repentance brings about change, not perfection. I knew that there had definitely been a change in me, so I concluded the problem was not that I had not truly repented. The four of us decided to spend some time in prayer about this after the evening program.

When we met for prayer, I admitted my sin of selfish ambition to God, and the others began to pray for me. When Danny prayed, God opened my eyes to why I battled with selfish ambition. Danny asked God to clearly show me the reason for my insecurities, questioning if it could be because of the way I grew up. When he said this, I knew immediately that this did have something to do with it. Danny thought perhaps it had something to do with my being the youngest of thirteen children. He knew that being the youngest, the things I said were generally considered stupid and my ideas were generally thought of as dumb. When I told stories or jokes, my siblings often were not interested or did not think they were funny. I knew I was very much loved by my brothers and sisters, but much of the time I felt like the baby sister who didn't know anything. I knew there was some truth in what

Danny thought, but it went even deeper than that. God was leading me to something else that had to do with the way I grew up.

Before I go on, let me explain the situation in which I grew up. My family was fairly poor, but that was not really what bothered me. What was very difficult for me to accept was that we lived in a messy house full of stuff with very junky surroundings. My parents had lived through the depression, and consequently had difficulty throwing things away. We lived in the country on 165 acres, and much of our land was covered with junk cars that my dad bought, thinking that some day he would be able to fix them up. The problem was that he bought more cars than he was able to fix, and eventually collected probably 300 or more. I was humiliated by this junk and did not want to bring my friends home for fear that they would not want to be my friends anymore. I was afraid they would view me as "white trash." I ran around with the popular girls at school because I thought more highly of them than other people, and I wanted people to associate me with them. In reality, I saw myself as lesser than other people because I did not have a nice, orderly house like I thought most people did.

After Danny prayed, Dave asked me if I could remember any times in the past, specifically in junior high (it was as if he knew), when I had been hurt or humiliated. I immediately thought of a particular incident in junior high when I traveled with my best friends to another town for a basketball game. Normally, when I did things with my friends, my mom would take me to town to meet them and would pick me up afterward. I could always avoid my friends' knowing where my house was because it was six miles from town. However, this time, because the dad of one of my friends was taking us to a game in a different town, I could not avoid his dropping me off at my house. On the way to the game, my friends kept pointing out junky houses and commenting that they couldn't see how people lived like that. The entire time I was thinking about the fact that on the way back, they were going to see my house, which was much junkier than any of the houses they were pointing out! Later, when we turned into our lane, I watched them all look around at the junk, and I sat in that car feeling humiliated by the way we lived.

When I told Dave and Danny this story, Dave asked me how I felt as I sat there. I told him I felt determined to prove to my friends that I was just as good as they were—in fact, that I was better, that I was more intelligent and more gifted. I also vowed that someday, when I would have my own house, I would keep it spotlessly clean and orderly. As I said these words to Dave, I realized that those decisions had built a stronghold of selfish ambition in my life. It really wasn't just this one incident that built the stronghold, but this incident was indicative of the way I reacted to the whole situation in which I grew up. As I related this story, we were in our prayer time with our eyes still shut. Dave then asked me if I could see Jesus in this situation. At this point my mind became confused, and I remember Dave stopping and asking God to bind Satan because it was evident we were dealing with a stronghold that Satan did not want to lose. Then it was as if I could see Jesus' arms around me, holding me in that car as I sat there.

As I felt His love for me, it didn't even bother me what my friends were thinking about me. Dave asked what He was saying to me, and it was as though I heard Him say, "That is not your house. Your house is in heaven, and it is a beautiful, immaculate mansion. You are my child, and that makes you a princess because I am a King." I realized that the girls in the car just did not know who I was! Dave asked me what I felt like saying to my friends now. I felt like I wanted to tell them that I really was a child of a King and that if they just knew him too, they could also be princesses. Suddenly, the competition I had felt turned into compassion and love for them.

After God gave me that mental picture of being in Christ's arms and hearing Him say that I am His child, Dave asked me if there were any verses that came to mind. The scriptures that God then gave me were the most significant thing that God used to help me during and after that time in prayer. The verses that I thought of were from John 15.

Making It Personal

Read the following verses from John 15:4-17 and answer the questions.

> Remain in me, and I will remain in you. No branch can bear fruit by itself; it must remain in the vine. Neither can you bear fruit unless you remain in me. I am the vine; you are the branches. If a man remains in me and I in him, he will bear much fruit; apart from me you can do nothing. (vv. 4-5)

1. How do we bear fruit? _____

2. Who is the source of our strength (the Vine)? _____

3. What are we able to produce apart from the Vine? _____

    > As the Father has loved me, so have I loved you. Now remain in my love. (v. 9)

    > The word *as* literally means "in the same manner," or could be translated "even as" or "like."

4. According to this verse, how much does Christ love us? _____
   _____

This is an amazing truth: Christ loves us as much as the Father loves Christ! You see, both God the Father's love and Christ's love are perfect, and consequently, Christ loves us every bit as much as the Father loves His Son! Perfect love cannot be improved upon.

5. What does it mean to *remain* in Christ's love? _____
_____

Strong's Exhaustive Concordance defines the Greek word translated *remain* in the NIV as "to stay (in a given place, state, relation or expectancy)."[1] To "remain in Christ's love," as I understand it, means to live mindful of His love, to allow myself to be wrapped in His loving arms and receive His love.

> My command is this: Love each other as [in the same manner] I have loved you. Greater love has no one than this, that he lay down his life for his friends. You are my friends if you do what I command. I no longer call you servants, because a servant does not know his master's business. Instead, I have called you friends, for everything that I learned from my Father I have made known to you. You did not choose me, but I chose you and appointed you to go and bear fruit—fruit that will last. Then the Father will give you whatever you ask in my name. This is my command: Love each other. (vv. 12-17)

6. We cannot love God or others until we grasp the incredible love Christ has for us. First John 4:7-8 says, "Dear friends, let us love one another, for love comes from God. Everyone who loves has been born of God and knows God." Why must we know God before we are able to love others?
_____
_____

When I "remain in Christ's love," I know that I am fully accepted, completely forgiven, valued, and delighted in; and knowing this truth gives me the ability to love others in the same way that I am experiencing Christ's love toward me.

Looking back, I believe I had attempted to repent of my sin previously without replacing the sin with Christ. I had not yet allowed Him to meet the real need of my heart because I had not yet found my value in Him. But the very next day, after that evening in prayer, I felt like a different person. I had peace and joy in my heart. I no longer felt the need to be recognized. I had no need to compete with others, prove myself, or flaunt my abilities. I felt free to love others and was not focused on myself. I had no battle with insecurity as long as I kept my focus on Christ because He viewed me as His princess! I had found a new source of strength and knew that I could do nothing apart from Christ. Knowing who I was in Christ had truly transformed me, and I have never been the same since.

I am not normally impacted by mental pictures. That experience in prayer was rather strange for me. It is usually the Word of God that speaks to me more than anything else; consequently, it was the verses themselves that spoke directly to me that night, especially where Jesus said, "Apart from me, you can do nothing." I realized that the reason I wasn't experiencing victory over my insecurities was because I wasn't staying connected to the Vine and drawing nourishment from Him. I had been trying to produce the fruit on my own, and that was not my job. My job was to stay connected to the Vine just like a fruitful branch must do, and the result would be much fruit. He didn't command me to bear fruit, He commanded me to remain in Him. Later, though, as I thought about it, I realized that the verses God gave me were the same as the picture He gave me: remaining in Christ's arms. Resting in His arms, I have the longings of my soul fulfilled, "and earth has nothing I desire besides [Him]" (Psalm 73:25).

As I meditated on John 15:12-17, I also saw that I could never love others as He has loved me if I were competing with them and seeking recognition. However, I began to experience the natural result of understanding His treasure in me: loving others as He had loved me!

One other significant thing happened that night. I had always felt condemned in my spirit for having these feelings of pride and insecurity. I felt that God was not pleased with me because of my sin. I realized that night that God had compassion for me in my helpless state, and He longed to meet the need of my soul, to let me know what a treasure I was to Him. The words of Psalm 103:13-14 were made alive to me that night: "As a father has compassion on his children, so the Lord has compassion on those who fear him; for He knows how we are formed, he remembers that we are dust."

Song for Worship and Meditation: "I Can See Your Love" sung and written by Leeland, from album *The Great Awakening*, 2011

Memory Verse

Remain in me, and I will remain in you. No branch can bear fruit by itself; it must remain in the vine. Neither can you bear fruit unless you remain in me. I am the vine; you are the branches. If a man remains in me and I in him, he will bear much fruit; apart from me you can do nothing. (John 15:4-5)

Going Deeper

Suggested Daily Schedule for Week 3

Day 1   Complete Lesson 3, "The Fruit of Insecurity."

Day 2   Complete Lesson 3, "The Root of Insecurity."

Day 3   Read 2 Peter 1:1-4; Romans 1:18-20, 28-31; 10:2-3; Jeremiah 9:23-24; Titus 3:3-7; Philippians 1:9-11; complete pages 134-137.

Day 4   Read John 15:1-17; complete pages 138-140.

Day 5   Read Ephesians 1-2; complete page 141.

Viewer Guide
Session 3: Christ's Call to Come

Jesus said to the Pharisees, "You diligently study the Scriptures because you think that by them you possess eternal life. These are the Scriptures that testify about me, yet you refuse to _____ ____ ____ to have life." (John 5:39-40)

Christ told the Pharisees that all the Old Testament Scriptures pointed to _____.

But the Pharisees refused to go to _____ in order to receive life.

Matthew 11:28-30

Jesus invites us to _____ ____ _____ and learn from _____ in order to find rest. It is because ____ _____ really is the fulfillment of all our needs!

Luke 18:9

The Pharisees were really looking to _____ to find life.

Matthew 23:1-4

The contrast between the Pharisees and Christ:

The Pharisees tied up _____ _____ and put them on men's shoulders (verse 4).

Christ said, "Come to me, all who are weary and burdened, and I will give you _____." **(**Matthew 11:28-29)

In Christ, we find _____.

John 6:35

_____ is the bread of life.

He said, "He who _____ ____ ____ will never go hungry, and he who_____ ____ ____ will never be thirsty."

John 7:37-38 says, "On the last and greatest day of the Feast, Jesus stood and said in a loud voice, 'If anyone is thirsty, let him _____ ____ ____ and drink. Whoever _____ ____ ____, as the Scripture has said, streams of living water will flow from within him."

In Christ we find _____.

In John 8:31-32, Jesus said, "If you hold to my teaching, you are really my disciples. Then you will know the _____, and the _____ will set you free."

Jesus said in John 14:6, "__ ____ the way and _____ _____ and the life."

In Christ we find _____.

Colossians 2:10 (NKJV) says that "you are complete in Him." This means that everything we lack, we have ____ _____!

In Christ we are _____.

Luke 19:1-10

In verse 5, Jesus told Zacchaeus, "Zacchaeus, _____ down immediately."

Second Corinthians 5:17 says, "Therefore, if anyone is in Christ, he is a new creation; the old has gone, the new has come!"

In Christ we are _____!

Mark 10:13-16

Mark 10:14 says, "When Jesus saw this, he was indignant. He said to them, 'Let the little children _____ ____ ____, and do not hinder them."

John 6:37 says, "All that the Father gives me will _____ ____ ____, and whoever _____ ____ ____ I will never drive away."

In Isaiah 55:1-3 the Lord says, "_____, all you who are thirsty, _____ to the waters; and you who have no money, _____, buy and eat! _____, buy wine and milk without money and without cost. Why spend money on what is not bread, and your labor on what does not satisfy? Listen, listen to me, and eat what is good, and your soul will delight in the richest of fare. Give ear and _____ ____ ____; hear me, that your soul may live. I will make an everlasting covenant with you, my faithful love promised to David."

Four

The Strength in Trusting

Christ began to show me that being free from the stronghold of selfish ambition required faith in His power to change me. To this point I had not really believed I would ever get victory. (If we listen to Satan's lie that we can never change, we will not change.) I had to believe that Christ had set me free and then act on that fact in faith. The same power that raised Christ from the dead can take a spiritually dead person and raise him to life. It gave me the ability to overcome a stronghold that had held me captive all of my life.

Making It Personal

1. Read Romans 6:4-7.

Do you believe that the same power that raised Christ from the dead can conquer the sin in your life and completely set you free from any stronghold? Yes / No

2. If you answered yes, express this belief to God in prayer. Write your prayer here so you can refer to it later in times of doubt or struggle. If you answered no, write out a prayer asking God to reveal to you by His Spirit and through His Word the extent of His power.

Trusting in God's Kindness and Compassion

Trusting in God's power alone to change me was not enough to transform me. But I found that trusting in His kindness and compassion automatically transformed me. I did not have to do anything to change. My new understanding of the character of God changed me!

> This is what the Sovereign Lord, the Holy One of Israel, says: "In repentance and rest is your salvation, in quietness and trust is your strength, but you would have none of it . . ." Yet the Lord longs to be gracious to you; he rises to show you compassion. For the Lord is a God of justice. Blessed are all who wait for him! . . . How gracious he will be when you cry for help! As soon as he hears, he will answer you . . . Whether you turn to the right or to the left, your ears will hear a voice behind you, saying, "This is the way; walk in it." Then you will defile your idols overlaid with silver and your images covered with gold; you will throw them away like a menstrual cloth and say to them, "Away with you!" (Isaiah 30:15, 18-22)

For me those idols were my selfish ambitions, but they had become as filthy as a menstrual cloth to me. I wrote in my Bible beside verse 22: "My selfish ambitions! Nov. 27, 2004." I began to desire no gods but the true and living God who loved me and gave Himself for me.

The reason this passage ministered so much to me was because God's compassion and kindness were what broke the stronghold of selfish ambitions in my life. You see, it is God's kindness that leads us to repentance, according to Romans 2:4. I realized for the first time that night in prayer at the conference in the Czech Republic that God was compassionate toward me *even in my sin* and longed to be gracious toward me and to meet the real needs of my heart. What transformed me was the fact that I saw that God's heart went out to me, that He wasn't angry with me for my insecurities and pride but that He was watching and waiting for me to run to Him to meet the longings of my soul! "How gracious he will be when you cry for help! As soon as he hears, he will answer you" (Isaiah 30:19).

I believe that the anger I had had toward my children was tied to the anger I thought God had toward me when I sinned. I had unrealistic expectations of my children because I thought God had unrealistic expectations of me. I thought my children were capable in themselves to do what I expected of them in the same way that I thought I must be capable in myself to do what God expected of me. When the children didn't live up to my expectations, I got angry with them and acted toward them in the same way that I thought God felt toward me when I sinned.

Knowing the truth about God's great love and acceptance—expressed through His compassion—made me into a different person. Without trying, I had no battle with insecurity. (I now knew my value as a child of God.) I had no need to compete with others. I had no need to prove myself or flaunt my abilities. I had a newfound capacity to love other people with the same love and compassion God had shown me. A power was broken that night by the way God dealt with me and by my discovering the truth about what God is like. This is not to say I have never since been tempted in those areas, but I now know to whom I can run to meet my needs. "For we do not have a high priest who is unable to sympathize with our weaknesses, but we have one who has been tempted in every way, just as we are—yet was without sin. Let us then approach the throne of grace *with confidence*, so that we may receive mercy and find grace to help us in our time of need" (Hebrews 4:15-16, emphasis added).

Making It Personal

1. Read Isaiah 30:15. This passage says that our salvation is in what two things?
   _____

In the same way that we were saved from sin at the moment we trusted Christ for our eternal salvation, we are saved from our daily sins as Christians by repenting and resting in what Christ has done for us.

2. According to this verse, in what two things is our strength?
   _____

This trust in God is what gives us strength over the power of sin.

3. Read Ephesians 6:10. This verse tells us that we need to find our power in whom? _____

4. Now read Ephesians 6:16. What is able to "extinguish all the flaming arrows of the evil one"?
   _____

5. It is our trust in a loving and powerful God that gives us strength over sin and Satan. Are you struggling with trusting and resting in His love for you? Yes / No

6. Remember, you cannot trust someone you do not know. How do you get to know God?
   _____

Romans 10:17 says, "Faith comes by hearing, and hearing *by the word of God*" (NKJV, emphasis added).

7. Read Isaiah 30:18-19, and notice the compassion in these verses.

   The Lord longs to be gracious to you; he rises to show you compassion . . . How gracious he will be when you cry for help! As soon as he hears, he will answer you.

Do you believe that God is compassionate toward you when you sin? This is important because what you believe about how God feels toward you is significantly tied to your struggle with sin. In fact, I believe that every area of sin we deal with is a result of not believing the truth about God. Satan is a liar and the father of lies (John 8:44).

8. The faith God desires of us involves more than just faith in His power to do great things. Read Matthew 15:21-28. In what attribute of Christ did the Canaanite woman believe that caused Him to heal her daughter? (Notice particularly verses 27-28.) _____
   _____

She trusted that God was not only offering salvation to the Jews. She believed He was a God of compassion who would also listen to her cries.

9. Read John 8:32. How did Jesus say you can be set free from sin? _____
   _____

Knowing the truth about God is our key to victory over sin, and the more we know Christ, the more we know God. (Colossians 1:15 tells us that Christ is "the image of the invisible God.") The more we *know* God, the more we are able to *trust* in who He is; and the more we trust in who He is, the less we are held captive by sin.

10. Read Hebrews 4:14-16 and fill in the missing words.

    Therefore, since we have a great high priest who has gone through the heavens, Jesus the Son of God, let us _____ _____ ___ _____ _____ ___ _____.
    For we do not have a high priest who is unable to_____ with our weaknesses, but we have one who has been tempted in every way, just as we are—yet was without sin. Let us then approach the throne of _____ with _____, so that we may receive _____ and find _____ to help us in our time of need.

The King James Version says, "For we have not an high priest who *cannot be touched* with the feeling of our infirmities" (emphasis added). I love that. He is touched with the feelings of my weakness. Consequently, I can approach His throne with confidence, knowing that I will "receive mercy and find grace to help in my time of need."

In what particular areas do you feel weak? _____
_____
_____
_____

How does it make you feel to know that Jesus' heart is compassionate toward your weakness?
_____

11. Fill in the blanks and answer the questions.

> But we ought always to thank God for you, brothers _____ by the Lord, because from the beginning God chose you to be saved through the sanctifying work of the Spirit and through _____ __ _____ _____. (2 Thessalonians 2:13)

Second Thessalonians 2:13 says that we are saved through two things. What are they?

_____
_____

> But the eyes of the Lord are on those who fear him, on those whose hope is in his _____ _____, to deliver them from death and keep them alive in famine. We wait ____ _____ for the Lord; he is our help and our shield. In him our hearts rejoice, for we _____ in his holy name. May your _____ _____ rest upon us, O Lord, even as we put our _____ in you. (Psalm 33:18-22)

Psalm 33:18-19 tells us that God comes to the rescue of those who fear Him and whose hope is in what? _____

Read Psalm 33:20-22 again and take some time to meditate on His compassion and unfailing love for you. Bask in the warmth of His love as you go about your life this week and trust in

His compassionate heart. You will be amazed at the transforming effect His unfailing love will have on you!

Song for Worship and Meditation: "In My Love," sung and written by Phil Wickham, bonus track from the album *Heaven & Earth (Expanded Edition)*, 2010

Memory Verse

For we do not have a high priest who is unable to sympathize with our weaknesses, but we have one who has been tempted in every way, just as we are—yet was without sin. Let us then approach the throne of grace with confidence, so that we may receive mercy and find grace to help us in our time of need. (Hebrews 4:15-16)

Going Deeper

Suggested Daily Schedule for Week 4

Day 1   Complete Lesson 4.

Day 2   Read Jeremiah 31:3; Isaiah 46:3-4; Isaiah 49:15; Hebrews 12:1-13; Isaiah 38:9, 17; Psalm 119:67-68; complete pages 142-143.

Day 3   Read Deuteronomy 31:6-8; Joshua 1:5-9; Psalm 27:1-3; 118:6-8; Isaiah 41:8-14; 43:1-7; 51:12-16; Matthew 28:19-20; Hebrews 13:5-6; complete pages 144-145.

Day 4   Read Isaiah 48:17-18, 22; 30:1-7, 15-19; 54:10; Psalm 16:1-2, 8; 112:6-8; 50:7-10; Isaiah 26:3-9; Psalm 90:14; complete pages 146-148.

Day 5   Read Psalm 34; complete pages 149-152.

Viewer Guide
Session 4: Trusting His Unfailing Love

I. Satan's Schemes

2 Corinthians 2:3-11

Verses 10-11

"If you forgive anyone, I also forgive him. And what I have forgiven—if there was anything to forgive—I have forgiven in the sight of Christ for your sake, in order that Satan might not outwit us. For we are not unaware of his _____."

Revelation 12:10 says that Satan is the _____ of the brethren.

Scheme #1: Satan _____ _____ ____ _____ in us so that we feel in bondage.

Luke 15:1-7
God's response to us when we become involved in sin is He _____ us.

Scheme #2: Satan seeks to keep us from understanding God's passionate pursuit to have the whole _____ of His children.

John 8:31-47
Scheme #3: Satan lies to us about who God is. He wants us to think that God is out to make our lives _____ or that we will be _____ _____ if we obey God and do not indulge the desires of our flesh.

At the root of sin is _____. We believe the lies of Satan and are led into sin.

Romans 12:1-2 says that we are not to be conformed to the world but to be transformed by the _____ of our minds. Then we will be able to understand what God's will is. We will understand that His will for us is _____, _____, and _____—it is the best for us.

II. Truth about God That Satan Doesn't Want Us to Know

Matthew 6:25-34

Truth #1: God deeply cares about us.

He cares about our _____ _____. Yet God sees things so much differently than we do. He is concerned with our deeper _____ needs far more than He is concerned with the less eternal needs such as the physical, material, and temporal needs that we think are so very important.

Hebrews 12:5-13

Truth #2: God can be trusted wholly and completely because His discipline is for our ____.

God does not desire to make our lives difficult, but rather to cause us to be transformed into humble, submissive lovers of Him who can truly satisfy the _____ of our soul—if we will but trust Him. "Man does not live on bread alone, but on _____ _____ that comes from the mouth of God." (Matthew 4:4)

Matthew 5:3-12. God's primary goal for us is to know and trust Him. If my circumstances cause me to know and trust God deeply, I am highly _____.

John 4:10 and 7:37-39

Truth #3: _____ _____ can fulfill all the longings of our souls.

Psalm 37:4 says, "Delight yourself in the LORD and ____ will give you the desires of your heart."

Five

The Power of God's Word

Not long after the conference I did the *Breaking Free* Bible study by Beth Moore. I had started it at some point previously, but it hadn't spoken to me at the time because I didn't believe I had any strongholds of sin resulting from my childhood. However, this time it came alive, and God greatly used it to show me the power of His Word to renew my mind. While doing the study, I made a list of the lies I believed had evolved into a stronghold of selfish ambition. Next to these lies I wrote down the truths from Scripture that God was using to set me free. I can still remember some of the things I wrote down. Here is a sampling:

Lies I Believed	**Truth That Can Set Me Free**
God has favorites.	"God does not show favoritism but accepts men from every nation who fear him and do what is right." (Acts 10:34-35) "Anyone who does wrong will be repaid for his wrong, and there is no favoritism." (Colossians 3:25)
People love me because of what I can do.	"Even 'sinners' love those who love them." (Luke 6:32) "What a man desires is unfailing love." (Proverbs 19:22)

I also wrote down verses that were helping me and put them up around the house. This helped me to meditate on truth. Whenever some thought or feeling would arise that was contrary to the truth of God's Word, I would refute the lie in my mind by reminding myself of the truth. God's Word began to renew my mind, and the lies lost their influence over me.

Making It Personal

Make a list of the lies you have believed, and next to each one write the truth of God's Word that refutes it. (If you need additional space for this exercise, there are additional pages for it in the "Going Deeper" section for Week 5, pp. 153-154.)

Lies I Believe   **Truth That Can Set Me Free**

I encourage you to take the list of verses you wrote down, copy them onto index cards, and place them around your house and your car, or wherever you will most often see them. Doing this helped me to "demolish arguments and every pretension that [set] itself up against the knowledge of God," and to "take captive every thought to make it obedient to Christ." (2 Corinthians 10:5)

One verse that became precious to me when I was doing the *Breaking Free* study was Psalm 45:10: "Listen, O daughter, consider and give ear: Forget your people and your father's house. The king is enthralled by your beauty; honor him, for he is your lord." On January 22, 2005, I wrote in my Bible next to this verse, "Following Mom's death, and also after being set free from the humiliation of the way I grew up, God gave me this verse." Meditating on this verse changed that inner feeling that I was "white trash" into the feeling that I was Christ's beautiful princess.

Jesus said, "If you hold to my teaching, you are really my disciples. Then you will know the truth, and the truth will set you free. . . . Now a slave has no permanent place in the family, but a son belongs to it forever. So if the Son sets you free, you will be free indeed" (John 8:31-32, 35-36). I am free indeed! The truth of His Word set me free! As I put the truth of God's Word in the place of the lies as they would come to my mind, God helped me to eventually get to the point of being able to talk about the things He had gifted me to do without feeling that those things made me better than others. As I replaced the lie of thinking I was better than others (Isn't it ironic that I believed this while also thinking of myself as "white trash"?), God transformed me into a person who sensed my need for the other members of the body of Christ. I began to see the unique value of every individual as a prized creation of God. This has been a process, and at times I still listen to the lies, but I now know where to go when I hear them. God has transformed my thinking, and He has changed me from the inside out. As long as I stay connected to the Vine, I do not struggle with insecurities, pride, or selfishness. Christ has become my dearest friend and the One whom I desire to exalt and live for.

Song for Worship and Meditation: "Show Us Christ," written by Doug Plank and Bob Sovereign, sung by Meghan Baird, from the album *The Gathering: Live from WorshipGod11*, 2011

Memory Verse

Choose a verse that you need to memorize to refute a lie you are prone to believe. You will have an opportunity to quote it to your prayer partner at the next session.

Going Deeper

Suggested Daily Schedule for Week 5

Day 1   Complete Lesson 5

Day 2-4 Rather than giving extra reading, I encourage you to complete the Making It Personal exercise. Search the Scriptures for passages that refute the lies you have believed. You may want to use a concordance, an online Bible tool, or a biblically knowledgeable friend to help you. Make a list of the lies you have believed, and next to each one write the truth of God's Word that refutes it. Space is provided for this exercise on pages 50, 153, and 154.

Day 5   Complete pages 155-156.

Viewer Guide
Session 5: The Power of God's Word

1. The Word of God is the means by which God the Father, Son, and Holy Spirit _____ _____ _____.

Psalm 33:6, 9
"By the _____ of the Lord were the heavens made, their starry host by the breath of his mouth."
Verse 9 says, "For he _____, and it came to be; he _____, and it stood firm."

In Genesis 1 we read how God _____ into existence physical life.

2. The Word of God is the means by which the Lord _____ _____ _____ _____.

Hebrews 1:3 says that Christ sustains "all things by his powerful _____."

Second Peter 3:5 says that "by God's _____ the heavens existed and the earth was formed out of water and by water." Verse 7 says, "By the same _____ the present heavens and earth are reserved for fire, being kept for the day of judgment and destruction of ungodly men."

3. The Word of God is the means by which the Spirit of God _____ _____ _____ _____ __ _____.

James 1:18
"He chose to give us birth through the _____ of truth."

1 Peter 1:23-25
"For you have been _____ _____, not of perishable seed, but of imperishable, through the living and enduring _____ ____ _____. For, 'All men are like grass, and all their glory is like the flowers of the field; the grass withers and the flowers fall, but the word of the Lord stands forever.' And this is the word that was preached to you."

First Peter 1:23-25 says the way in which we received spiritual life was through the _____ ____ _____ being _____ in us.

Jesus told a parable, recorded in Matthew 13, Mark 4, and Luke 8 that compared the word of God to _____ planted by a farmer. First Peter 1:23-25 says that those who have been spiritually born again are spiritually given life by the imperishable _____ of the Word of God.

John 6:63
"The Spirit gives life; the flesh counts for nothing. The words I have spoken to you are spirit and they are life."
Christ's words are _____ and _____.

In John 3:3, 5 Jesus said, "I tell you the truth, no one can see the kingdom of God unless he is born again. . . I tell you the truth, no one can enter the kingdom of God unless he is born of water and the Spirit."
Jesus said we must be born of _____ and the _____.

Titus 3:3-5
"At one time we too were foolish, disobedient, deceived and enslaved by all kinds of passions and pleasures. We lived in malice and envy, being hated and hating one another. But when the kindness and love of God our Savior appeared, he saved us, not because of righteous things we had done, but because of his mercy. He saved us through the _____ of _____ and _____ by the _____ _____."

John 15:1-3
"I am the true vine, and my Father is the gardener. He cuts off every branch in me that bears no fruit, while every branch that does bear fruit he _____ so that it will be even more fruitful. You are already _____ because of the _____ I have spoken to you."
Jesus said the disciples had become clean through the _____ that He had spoken to them.

Ephesians 5:25-27
"Husbands, love your wives, just as Christ loved the church and gave himself up for her to make her holy, cleansing her by the washing with water through the word, and to present her to himself as a radiant church, without stain or wrinkle or any other blemish, but holy and blameless."
Christ has cleansed us by _____ us with _____ through the _____.

4. The Word of God is the means by which the Spirit of God _____ _____ _____.

Jesus said in Matthew 4:4, "Man does not live on bread alone, but on _____ _____ that comes from the mouth _____ _____."

In the same way that food is necessary for physical life, _____ _____ ____ _____ is necessary to keep us nourished spiritually.

First Peter 2:2-3, "Like newborn babies, crave _____ _____ _____, so that by it you may grow up in your salvation, now that you have _____ that the _____ is _____."

First Thessalonians 2:13 says, "And we also thank God continually because, when you received the word of God, which you heard from us, you accepted it not as the word of men, but as it actually is, the _____ ____ _____, which is at work in you who believe."

How is the Word of God at work in us to sustain us spiritually?

John 17:17
"Sanctify them by the _____; your word is _____."

James 1:21 says, "Get rid of all moral filth and the evil that is so prevalent and _____ accept the _____ _____ in you, which can _____ you."

Why do we need to be sanctified by the truth of God's Word?

    1.) We need to be sanctified by truth because of the _____ of our own _____ _____.

James 1:13-16
"When tempted, no one should say, 'God is tempting me.' For God cannot be tempted by evil, nor does he tempt anyone; but each one is tempted when, by _____ _____ _____ _____, he is dragged away and enticed. Then, after desire has conceived, it gives birth to sin; and _____, when it is full-grown, _____ _____ to _____. Don't be deceived, my dear brothers."

Sin produces _____ in us, but the word of God produces _____ in us!

Hebrews 3:13 says that we need to "encourage one another daily" so that none of us will be hardened by _____ _____."

Colossians 3:16
"Let the _____ of _____ dwell in you richly, teaching and admonishing one another in all wisdom, singing psalms and hymns and spiritual songs, with thankfulness in your hearts to God."

    2.) We need to be sanctified by truth because of the _____ of _____.

The Word of God is called the _____ ____ _____ _____ in Ephesians 6.

Hebrews 4:12
"For the _____ ____ _____ is _____ and active. Sharper than any double-edged _____, it penetrates even to dividing soul and spirit, joints and marrow; it judges the thoughts and attitudes of the heart."

    3.) We need to be sanctified by truth because of the _____ of what _____ _____ has to offer.

Jesus said that "the one who received the seed that fell among the thorns is the man who hears the word, but the worries of this life and the deceitfulness of wealth choke it, making it unfruitful" (Matthew 13:22). The _____ of _____ _____ and the _____ of _____ choked out the seed of the word that was planted in this man.

Jeremiah 15:16
"When your _____ came, I ate them; they were my joy and my heart's delight, for I bear your name, LORD God Almighty."

John 1:1 calls Jesus the _____ ____ _____.

Hebrews 1:1-2
"In the past God spoke to our forefathers through the prophets at many times and in various ways, but in these last days he has spoken to us by his Son, whom he appointed heir of all things, and through whom he made the universe."
Jesus is called the Word of God because _____ has _____ to us _____ _____.

John 15:7
"If you remain in me and ____ _____ _____ ____ _____, ask whatever you wish, and it will be given you."

1 John 2:14
"I write to you, young men, because you are strong, and the _____ of _____ _____ ____ _____, and you have overcome the evil one."

The word of God is not like vitamins, it is a _____ _____!

His Third Wooing

Lavishing His Grace on Me

I delight greatly in the Lord;
my soul rejoices in my God.
For He has clothed me with garments of salvation
and arrayed me in a robe of righteousness,
as a bridegroom adorns his head like a priest,
and as a bride adorns herself with her jewels.

Isaiah 61:10

Six

Awakened to Grace

I had heard Christ wooing me to give Him all of myself. It was as if He had taken my face into His hands and caused me to gaze on Him and Him alone. He had called me His princess. He had taken me into His arms and loved me. But He was not done with me. I had only begun to grasp His incredible love for me. I still struggled; the old Clara sometimes came out. Whenever I got angry, desired to be recognized, or dealt with other familiar sins, I felt that God was displeased with me, that I had failed Him even after all He had taught me. And I thought my failure caused Him to turn His back toward me.

Why did I still find myself dealing with these same old things when Christ had set me free from them?

I had allowed Christ to hold me in His arms, *but I still had not learned to rest there*. I could not see that I was still striving to produce my own righteousness, to get rid of sin in my life so that I might be pleasing to God. Somehow I could not embrace the fact that Christ had already done all the work of saving me from my sin when He died on the cross. I battled back and forth with my sinful nature, and seemingly experienced times of victory only to be followed by times of defeat. I really lived a performance-based Christian life, feeling God was pleased with me as long as I was having spiritual victory, but feeling defeat and discouragement when I failed. I experienced what some have called "roller-coaster Christianity."

I must have somehow communicated this up-and-down struggle to a fellow missionary because he gave me a magazine article on grace. I read the article and wondered to myself why he thought I needed to read it. I agreed with everything that was written in the article; however, the fact that he thought I needed it jarred my attention.

I remember Danny making a remark about God always smiling down on us, and I reacted to that because I did not believe God always smiled down on *me*. I also remember talking with another Christian friend about the fact that though I was trying to please God and not men and had gotten some victory in this area, I knew there were times I still longed for the approval of people. My friend tried to tell me that God was already pleased with me simply because I was His child, but I used many verses to argue that He wasn't necessarily pleased or He wouldn't command us to live to please Him. Here are some of those verses:

So we make it our goal to please him, whether we are at home in the body or away from it. For we must all appear before the judgment seat of Christ, that each one may receive what is due him for the things done while in the body, whether good or bad. (2 Corinthians 5:9-10)

An unmarried man is concerned about the Lord's affairs—how he can please the Lord. (1 Corinthians 7:32)

Am I now trying to win the approval of men, or of God? Or am I trying to please men? If I were still trying to please men, I would not be a servant of Christ. (Galatians 1:10)

Finally, brothers, we instructed you how to live in order to please God, as in fact you are living. Now we ask you and urge you in the Lord Jesus to do this more and more. (1 Thessalonians 4:1)

No one serving as a soldier gets involved in civilian affairs—he wants to please his commanding officer. (2 Timothy 2:4)

I now believe that Satan was twisting these verses in my thinking, trying to make me believe that it was my duty to please God.

Years prior to this, I had read a book called *Grace* by Lewis Sperry Chafer, and I remember being impressed with the fact that it is pride that causes people to be prone to produce their own righteousness and makes them think they can do for God what He alone can do. I realized at that time that this is why lost people have a hard time coming to Christ for their eternal salvation. However, I never realized that this was exactly what I was doing in trying to be saved from sin on a daily basis.

Around this time, I noticed that the missionary friend who had given me the article on grace also had the book *Grace Awakening* by Charles Swindoll, and I asked if I could borrow it. This book begins by alerting the reader to the fact that Satan has perverted the gospel through legalism. It echoes what Paul was saying to the Galatians:

> You foolish Galatians! Who has bewitched you? Before your very eyes Jesus Christ was clearly portrayed as crucified. I would like to learn just one thing from you: Did you receive the Spirit by observing the law, or by believing what you have heard? Are you so foolish? After beginning with the Spirit, are you now trying to attain your goal by human effort? (Galatians 3:1-3)

Swindoll drives home the fact that trying to gain acceptance with God by any set of rules and regulations is a doctrine of demons to get the focus on us rather than on Christ.

I did not fully see that I was still trying to gain acceptance with God by my own set of rules until God gave me a firsthand illustration. For our twentieth wedding anniversary, Danny took me to Greece for a week-long vacation. He was able to get a flight from Vienna (our nearest international airport) to Athens very inexpensively, but once we got there we discovered that everything was quite a bit more expensive than in Slovakia. All week he was spending money in order to make our time memorable. We are both normally frugal, so I thought he was being unusually lavish with me. In spite of his generosity, however, I did not feel loved. In fact, I was feeling insecure because we spent a substantial amount of time on the beach where women were not dressed very modestly. I convinced myself that Danny was probably comparing my body to these women. (It didn't help that my body bore the marks of childbearing, so I was already feeling unattractive.)

At the end of the week, he topped off his generosity by taking me on a cruise. We hadn't been on board long when I felt compelled to talk to him about the fact that he didn't know how to meet my needs and that he seldom told me that he thought I was attractive. (I know, it was a very inappropriate time, but I was intensely struggling on the inside.) After spilling my feelings, I realized I had hurt him deeply. He is not one to display emotion, but after having lived with him for twenty years, I knew when he was angry and hurt. He said to me, "I took you to Greece for our anniversary. I've been spending money on you all week, and now I'm taking you on a cruise . . . and you don't feel like I show you that I love you?!"

I didn't know what to do or say, so I got my *Grace Awakening* book and started reading it again. As I read, I felt like God said to me, "You just don't get it, do you? I love you! I sent my Son to *die* for you to make you totally pure in my sight, and you still feel like I am not pleased with you?" I went over to Danny with tears streaming down my face and thanked him for being an illustration to me of a God who loves me unconditionally just the way I am, a God to whom I do not have to prove anything, a God who loves me and accepts me because I am His. I am beautiful to Him, not because of what I try to do for Him but because "Christ loved [me] and gave himself up for [me] to make [me] holy, cleansing [me] by the washing with water through the word . . . to present [me] to himself as a radiant [bride], without stain or wrinkle or any other blemish, but holy and blameless" (Ephesians 5:25-27).

Making It Personal

1. Read Ephesians 5:25-27. In your own words, describe how God sees you. _____

   _____

   _____

   _____

   _____

   _____

Do you *truly* believe God sees you this way, or are you still trying to make yourself presentable to Him? _____

If you feel you are trying to make yourself presentable to Him, how do you normally do this?
_____
_____

2. Read Hebrews 9:24-28. How many times has Christ had to sacrifice Himself to do away with sin? _____

3. Read Hebrews 10:1-23. Through the sacrifice of Christ's body, what have we been made (v. 10)? _____

What did Christ do after he offered himself as a sacrifice for sins (v. 12)? _____
This signifies His work was finished.

What has He done for those who are being made holy (v. 14)? _____

For how long (v. 14)? _____

4. Do you have confidence and full assurance of faith when you go to God in prayer, or do you feel you have to get your act together first, get your sin confessed, and make sure there is nothing between you and God before He will listen to you? _____

_____

If you feel you still have to do something, you are saying that Christ's finished work was not enough to make you acceptable to God and to save you from your daily sins. You may trust it was enough to save you from the penalty of hell, but you feel it is your responsibility to still do something in order to receive forgiveness on a continual basis.

5. Read Colossians 2:13-23. How many sins did God forgive us of (v. 13)? _____ (Notice also the past tense of the verb.)

What did God do with "the written code [the law] . . . that was against us" (v. 14?
_____
_____

The law proved our guilt. Usually the Romans nailed the list of wrongdoings for which a criminal was crucified to his cross. God showed that our debt was fully paid by Christ's death and that the law was canceled when he nailed it to the cross.

6. Read Hebrews 4:14-16. How are we to approach the throne of grace? _____
_____

Notice verse 15. The reason we can approach the throne boldly is because we have a _____ _____ who understands our weaknesses because He too lived in an earthly body and dealt with temptation. Satan wants us to think we have to get our act together before we can go to the throne because he knows that the only way we can overcome temptation is by going to God for help. If we think we cannot get to God because He is displeased that we are being drawn to sin, we will try to fight the temptation on our own, and we are sure to fall!

7. Read Romans 8:8. Why is it a true statement to say that we cannot please God by overcoming sin? _____
_____

God is not pleased with us for overcoming sin because He knows it is impossible for us to do that! *He* is the one who has overcome sin in our lives by His finished work on the cross.

8. Read Hebrews 11:5-6. What is the only way we can please God? _____

If our sinful nature cannot please God, why would God expect us to do something impossible? He doesn't! He simply wants us, by faith, to come boldly to the throne of grace and find mercy and grace to help us in our time of need, and then He does the work for us. It is that simple. We make it complicated because we are so prone to want to do the work ourselves.

> Therefore, there is now no condemnation for those who are in Christ Jesus, because through Christ Jesus the law of the Spirit of life set me free from the law of sin and death. For what the law was powerless to do in that it was weakened by the sinful nature, God did by sending his own Son in the likeness of sinful man to be a sin offering. And so he condemned sin in sinful man, in order that the righteous requirements of the law might be fully met in us, who do not live according to the sinful nature but according to the Spirit. (Romans 8:1-4)

Song for Worship and Meditation: "Grace," sung and written by Phil Wickham, recorded as a single, 2006

Memory Verse

Therefore, there is now no condemnation for those who are in Christ Jesus, because through Christ Jesus the law of the Spirit of life set me free from the law of sin and death. (Romans 8:1-2)

Going Deeper

Suggested Daily Schedule for Week 6

Day 1 Complete Lesson 6

Day 2 Read Psalm 86:11; Hebrews 3:7-4:16; Psalm 103:7-18; Exodus 33:12-34:7; Psalm 25:4-10; complete pages 157-160.

Day 3 Read Romans 3; complete pages 161-162.

Day 4 Read Romans 4; complete pages 163-164.

Day 5 Read Galatians 3; complete pages 165-167.

Viewer Guide
Session 6: Clothed with Christ's Righteousness

Isaiah 64:6

"All of us have become like one who is unclean, and all our righteous acts are like filthy rags; we all shrivel up like a leaf, and like the wind our sins sweep us away."

Zechariah 3:1-5

Joshua was the _____ _____ (v. 1).

He was standing before _____ _____ ____ _____ _____ (_____) (vv. 1-2).

Joshua's clothes were _____(v. 3).

_____ was standing at Joshua's right side, accusing him (v. 1).

Revelation 12:10 calls Satan "the _____ of the _____."

The Lord _____ Satan, saying that Joshua was a _____ _____ snatched from the _____ (Zechariah 3:2).

Christ told those standing before Him to take off _____ _____ _____(v. 4).

The filthy clothes represented _____ _____ (v. 4).

_____ told Joshua that _____ had taken away Joshua's sin (v. 4).

Christ said He would _____ _____ _____ ____ _____ (v. 4).

A _____ _____ was put on Joshua's head.

Ephesians 5:25-27 "Husbands, love your wives, just as Christ loved the church and gave himself up for her to make her _____, _____ her by the _____ with water through the word, and to present her to himself as a _____church, without stain or wrinkle or any other blemish, but _____ and _____."

Revelation 19:7-8

"'Let us rejoice and be glad and give him glory! For the wedding of the Lamb has come, and his bride has made herself ready._____ _____, _____ and _____, _____ _____ ___ to wear.' (Fine linen stands for the _____ acts of the saints.)"

Psalm 45:13-14: "All glorious is the princess within her chamber; her gown is _____ with _____. In _____ _____ she is led to the king."

Isaiah 61:10 says, "I delight greatly in the LORD; my soul rejoices in my God. For he has clothed me with garments of _____ and arrayed me in a robe of _____, as a bridegroom adorns his head like a priest, and as a _____ _____ herself with her_____."

Isaiah describes the "embroidered garments" of Psalm 45:14, the "rich garments" and "white turban" of Zechariah 3:4, and the "fine linen, bright and clean" of Revelation 19:8 that Christ clothes us with as garments of _____ and as a robe of _____.

"Find rest, O my soul, in God alone; my hope comes from him. He alone is my rock and my salvation; he is my fortress, I will not be shaken." (Psalm 62:5-6)

_____ _____ is our salvation (v. 6).

Romans 4:4-5

"Now when a man works, his wages are not credited to him as a gift, but as an obligation. However, to the man who does not work but trusts God who justifies the wicked, his faith is credited as _____."

We receive this "clothing" of righteousness by _____ in Christ's sacrificial death on the cross for us.

Revelation 12:11 says that we overcome Satan's accusations by the _____ of the Lamb.

Hebrews 11:28 tells us that the sacrificed lamb's _____ on the doorposts of the Israelites' houses kept the destroyer of the firstborn not to touch the firstborn of Israel.

When Satan is accusing us, it is _____ that the _____ of Christ has covered our sins that causes Satan to flee to flee from us. (1 Peter 5:9, James 4:7)

Seven

Enlightened to God's Great Power

My dear sister,

> I keep asking that the God of our Lord Jesus Christ, the glorious Father, may give you the Spirit of wisdom and revelation, so that you may know him better. I pray also that the eyes of your heart may be enlightened in order that you may know the hope to which he has called you, the riches of his glorious inheritance in the saints, and his incomparably great power for us who believe. That power is like the working of his mighty strength, which he exerted in Christ when he raised him from the dead. (Ephesians 1:17–20)

As I began to understand the finished work of Christ for me, I gained a new understanding of the doctrine of salvation. I had always been taught that there is a "positional righteousness" (justification) that God gives us at the moment we receive Christ—that makes us as though we had never sinned—and that there is also a "practical righteousness" (sanctification) that develops as we mature in our faith. I had understood—I should say misunderstood—this practical righteousness to mean that I had to work out my own salvation on a daily basis. I trusted God for my positional righteousness, but in my heart I believed it was up to me to obtain my practical righteousness, or salvation from the power of sin over me. This lie I had believed had been evidenced by the following:

- A lack of power. I found that I could not make myself more pleasing to God. I was trying to do what was impossible to do. (I think the reason we are prone to try to do this is because we want to feel good about ourselves.)

- A lack of joy. I found that I had no joy because the Christian life was about striving to please God rather than resting in what He had already done for me and enjoying Him.
- A lack of peace. Whenever I sinned, I found that I was plagued by condemnation, a feeling of shame, and a feeling that God was displeased with me. I would also be defensive when people pointed out my weaknesses because I felt as though I had to prove that I was not so bad.
- A lack of love. I found myself being judgmental toward others. I have since learned that any time I am judgmental of others, it is a sign that I have forgotten who it is that makes me righteous and the compassion that He extends to me in my helplessness.

Making It Personal

1. Think about the evidences I just listed. Check each one that you see in your own life.

    ☐ Lack of power
    ☐ Lack of joy
    ☐ Lack of peace
    ☐ Lack of love

Now consider some of the scriptures that helped me to come to a clearer understanding of what Christ did for me at the cross in not only providing salvation from hell (both the guilt and penalty of sin), but salvation from sin itself.

2. Read Colossians 2:1-23. How did you receive Christ Jesus as Lord (vv. 6-7)? _____

3. Verses 6-7 mention three specific ways in which we are to continue to live in Christ. These three ways are:

_____

_____

_____

The Colossians passage gave me a clear understanding that in the same way I received Christ Jesus at the point of salvation, I was to live the Christian life: depending completely on Him to save me from sin, being strengthened by Him in faith, and overflowing with thankfulness. The Christian life is about *Him* and His power to save us, not about our trying through human effort to be like Him.

In his book, *Transforming Grace*, Jerry Bridges writes:

> All too often we who are believers living in the realm of grace, live out our daily lives as if we were still living under the bondage of the law . . . I am convinced that the sinful nature still present within every believer tends toward a legalistic spirit as much as it tends toward sin. The sinful nature despises the righteousness that comes by faith in Jesus Christ as much as it despises the ethical righteousness that comes from obeying God's law. If we are going to serve in the newness of the Spirit, we must resist the legalistic spirit of trying to "live by the law" as vigorously and persistently as we do temptations to sin.[2]

If I am constantly striving to do all the right things to please God, I will never find joy and peace because I can never do all the right things. I know that very well. I fully relate to the Jews Paul talked about in Romans 10:3: "Since they did not know the righteousness that comes from God and sought to establish their own, they did not submit to God's righteousness." My efforts to make myself righteous interfered with God living His righteousness through me. But verse 4 goes on to say, "Christ means the end of the struggle for righteousness" (Phillips). Hallelujah!

Soon after we moved back to the United States and began attending The Summit Church (North Little Rock, Ark.), Life Action Ministries held a revival crusade in our church. During the crusade, I began to be plagued in my conscience by some sins that I felt I had to confess to someone but at the same time, for some reason, did not have peace about doing so. I could not get any peace of mind over this matter. Satan was really doing a number on me until, as I was reading my Bible one morning in Hebrews 11, I came to verse 28: "By faith [Moses] kept the Passover and the sprinkling of blood, so that the destroyer of the firstborn would not touch the firstborn of Israel." God tenderly spoke to my heart and showed me that Christ's blood had already been sprinkled on me to cleanse my conscience. I just needed to accept it by faith, and there was nothing else for me to do in order to receive forgiveness.‡ Faith in the blood of Christ to cover my sin caused Satan to flee. I wept as I was relieved of a burden that had been bothering me for days.

---

‡ Of course there are times when we need to go to a person whom we have wronged and ask their forgiveness, but that was not the case in this instance.

Making It Personal

1. Read 1 Peter 5:8-9 and Luke 22:31-32. According to these passages, what is necessary in order for Satan to flee from us? _____

2. Read Revelation 12:10-11. It says that Satan is "the accuser of the brothers, who accuses them before our God day and night," but they overcome him "by _____ _____ _____ _____ _____ and by the word of their testimony."

For me, confessing my sin to others had become my "penance" in order to feel as though I had done something to make up for the sin. In fact, confessing my sin to God had also become a ritual I believed I must go through in order to receive forgiveness. The Christian life had been about regulations for me, and this was one of them (the ritual of confession) that still burdened me. After all, didn't 1 John 1:9 say that "if we confess our sins, he is faithful and just and will forgive us our sins and purify us from all unrighteousness"? And didn't Psalm 66:18 say, "If I regard iniquity in my heart, the Lord will not hear me" (KJV)? For me this meant that I had to do something in order to receive forgiveness or for God to hear me, and that something was confession. But I was learning that my view of 1 John 1:9 and Psalm 66:18 was not compatible with what the rest of Scripture teaches about the finished work of Christ. Confession is not a ritual we go through in order to receive forgiveness. We have already been forgiven for all our sins—past, present, and future (Colossians 2:13). If our forgiveness as Christians were dependent upon our confession, then receiving forgiveness would be dependent upon us. We *have* (present tense) the forgiveness of sins *through Christ's blood* (Colossians 1:14; Ephesians 1:7).

The literal meaning of the Greek word for *forgive* in 1 John 1:9 is "to send off" or "to send away." I do not believe the intent of this verse is to put us under the obligation of a ritual of confession, but rather to help us understand that when we do sin, if we will agree with God about the truth of our sin, He will send the sin away. In other words, *He* (rather than we) will deal with the sin. We do not have to fight it on our own and try to get our act together before going to God. We simply admit our weakness in the same way that we received salvation in the first place when we accepted Christ, and He is faithful and just to send the sin away and to purify us from all unrighteousness. The purpose of confession is to stop sin or to cause us to turn from our sin; confession is not our way of making up for it.

This new understanding gave me a fresh appreciation for my Savior. I no longer felt condemned when I sinned. I felt His compassion and love to help me forsake the sin. And when I admitted my weakness, He gave me the power to overcome the sin. Now when I sin, I know I need to go to Him to meet the deeper need of my heart that drove me to the sin in the first place. Jesus gave us a true picture of this in the way He dealt with the tax collectors and sinners, in the way He dealt with the woman caught in adultery, and in the story He told about the father of the prodigal son who ran to his son as soon as he saw him coming home for help.

James 4:6-10 explains it so beautifully:

> But he gives us more grace. That is why Scripture says: "God opposes the proud but gives grace to the humble." Submit yourselves, then, to God. Resist the devil, and he will flee from you. Come near to God and he will come near to you. Wash your hands, you sinners, and purify your hearts, you double-minded. Grieve, mourn and wail. Change your laughter to mourning and your joy to gloom. Humble yourselves before the Lord, and he will lift you up.

God cannot help the proud because the proud refuse to be helped. They are trying to overcome sin in their own strength. We have to admit our weakness and inability to overcome the sin before we can be given the grace to overcome it.

To quote Lewis Sperry Chafer,

> Every human work . . . which is wrought with a view to meriting acceptance with God, is of the nature of a legal covenant of works, and therefore, belongs only to the law. Through the finished work of Christ, acceptance with God is perfectly secured; but that acceptance can be experienced only through a faith which turns from dependence on merit, and rests in Christ as the sufficient Savior . . . Any manner of life, or service, which is lived in dependence on the flesh, rather than in dependence on the Spirit, is legal in character.[3]

Galatians 5:18 says, "If you are led by the Spirit, you are not under law." Do you see how Satan had so cunningly confused me? Confession had become a form of working to be accepted by God. Satan will choose any method he can to get the focus on us instead of Christ.

Making It Personal

1. Do you feel the need to make sure that there is no sin in your life and that your sins are confessed before God will listen to you? Yes / No

If you feel that everything must be right between you and God and that you must have all sin confessed for Him to hear you, what if you are in the act of sinning and want out, but are powerless to stop? What do you do then?

2. Is the purpose of confession to gain acceptance with God? Yes / No

If not, what is its purpose? _____

3. Read Hebrews 4:14-16 and fill in the blanks.

> Therefore, since we have a great high priest who has gone through the heavens, _____ _____ _____ ____ _____, let us hold firmly to the _____ we profess. For we do not have a high priest who is unable to _____ with our _____, but we have one who has been tempted in every way, just as we are—yet was without sin. Let us then approach the throne of grace _____ _____, so that we may receive _____ and find _____ to help us in our time of need.

Admitting our sin to God and asking for help is our power to overcome it!

4. Psalm 66:18 was a verse that had confused me about the need for confession. In the King James Version it says, "If I regard iniquity in my heart, the Lord will not hear me." Read Psalm 66:16-20 in the NIV. What does the psalmist say would have kept the Lord from listening to his prayer?
_____

Psalm 66:18 does not teach that when we sin, God turns away from us and refuses to listen to us until we get ourselves cleaned up. God is ready to hear the prayer of anyone who calls out to Him in prayer for help to overcome sin, and that is what confession is—admitting our need for help.

Read also James 4:1-3. Why do these verses say that we at times do not receive what we ask for?
_____

It is when we ask with wrong motives that God will not give us what we are asking. We cannot expect God to give us what we want if we are cherishing sin, as Psalm 66:18 says, because then it would be as though God were giving His stamp of approval to our sin. He purposely creates adverse circumstances to get us to repent, not out of anger, but by way of discipline.

5. Read Hebrews 12:5-13. What is God's purpose in disciplining us? _____
_____

6. Read Proverbs 3:11-12. In what way does the Lord discipline us? "... as a father the son _____ _____ __."

If your parents disciplined you in anger, you have not gotten a true picture of the way God deals with His children. First Thessalonians 5:9 says, "For God did not appoint us to suffer wrath but to receive salvation through our Lord Jesus Christ." I'm convinced Satan accuses us and makes us feel that God is angry with us because he knows we will not turn for help to a God whom we believe has turned His back on us in indignation.

7. Read Ephesians 2:1-10. How are we saved (v. 8)? _____

As a Christian, do you feel the need to gain God's approval or appease him? Yes / No
If so, ask God to give you an understanding of the finished work of Christ and the grace that He has offered to you. Grace is God's giving to us what we do not deserve. He has freely given us salvation, and we do not *owe* Him anything!

Why do you think it is that we are so prone to want to merit God's favor (v. 9)? _____
_____

Chafer explains the problem of trying to repay God this way:

> All attempts to repay His gift, be they ever so sincere, serve only to frustrate His grace and to lower the marvelous kindness of God to the sordid level of barter and trade. How faithfully we should serve Him, but never to repay Him! Service is the Christian's means of expressing his love and devotion to God, as God has expressed His love to those whom He saves by the gracious thing He has done. Christian service for God should be equally gracious.[4]

When we serve God with the motive of receiving His acceptance or favor in return, we are not serving Him graciously, but we are serving Him legalistically. Understanding God's grace is vital to serving God in freedom.

What do you think verse 10 means when it says that we were "created in Christ Jesus to do good works"?
_____

8. Read Ephesians 3:20-21. Whose power is at work within us and is able to do "immeasurably more than all we ask or imagine"? _____

Who alone deserves glory (v. 21)? _____

9. Read Philippians 2:12-13. Where do we get both the desire and the power to do works pleasing to God? _____

God *has* called us to do good works through *His* power. However, the Christian life is not about focusing on bettering ourselves by doing works pleasing to God; it is about a relationship with a mighty God who is at work in us to change us. This is why Titus 2:11-14 says,

> For the grace of God that brings salvation has appeared to all men. It teaches us to say "No" to ungodliness and worldly passions, and to live self-controlled, upright and godly lives in this present age, while we wait for the blessed hope—the glorious appearing of our great God and Savior, Jesus Christ, who gave himself for us to redeem us from all wickedness and to purify for himself a people that are his very own, eager to do what is good.

I do not believe that grace and truth are contradictions that need to be in balance. Rather, this verse teaches that grace *is* the truth that sets us free from sin! *Christ* is the one at work in us doing immeasurably more than we could ask or imagine to save us from sin and to transform us into His image. We work out our salvation from sin on a daily basis by relying on Christ alone. Apart from Him we can do nothing.

Song for Worship and Meditation: "Savior, Please," sung and written by Josh Wilson, from the album *Trying To Fit the Ocean in a Cup*, 2008

Memory Verse

For the grace of God that brings salvation has appeared to all men. It teaches us to say "No" to ungodliness and worldly passions, and to live self-controlled, upright and godly lives in this present age, while we wait for the blessed hope—the glorious appearing of our great God and Savior, Jesus Christ, who gave himself for us to redeem us from all wickedness and to purify for himself a people that are his very own, eager to do what is good. (Titus 2:11-14)

Going Deeper

Suggested Daily Schedule for Week 7

Day 1   Complete Lesson 7.

Day 2   Read Hebrews 9; complete pages 168-169.

Day 3   Read Hebrews 10:1-25; complete pages 170-172.

Day 4   Read Romans 2; complete pages 173-175.

Day 5   Read Galatians 3:26-5:16; complete pages 176-179.

Viewer Guide
Session 7: Evidences of Not Resting in Christ

1. Trusting in ourselves instead of in Christ is evidenced by a lack of _____.

Romans 10:1-4

The Israelites were not able to submit to God's righteousness because _____ _____ _____ _____ _____ _____ _____.

The Israelites were zealous for _____. Their zeal was not based on _____. They did not understand that _____ _____ _____ _____ and that only _____ could make them righteous.

They were seeking to establish their own righteousness because "they did not know the _____ that comes from _____."

God is not disappointed in you for your inability to do what is right because He knows you are completely _____ apart from Him to do anything right.

Romans 5:8

"But God demonstrates his own love for us in this: While we were still sinners, Christ died for us."
What is true for lost sinners is true for us saved sinners as well: God showed His compassion toward us helpless sinners by sending Christ to die for us and to save us from sin's power.

Romans 10:4 says, "Christ is the end of the law so that there may be righteousness for everyone who _____.

Not only are we declared righteous at the moment we trust Christ for our eternal salvation, but the way we live righteous lives of obedience as Christians is *also* by _____.

Romans 1:17

"For in the gospel a righteousness from God is revealed, a righteousness that is _____ _____ _____ _____ _____ _____, just as it is written: 'The righteous will live _____ _____.'"

If we lack the power to gain victory over sin, we can conclude that we lack _____ in who God is and what He has done for us and that we are not _____ _____ _____ to save us from the sin but are _____ _____ _____ _____.

So how do we get faith?

Romans 10:17 says that "faith comes from hearing the message, and the message is heard through the word of Christ." The _____ ____ _____ is what increases our faith.
Freedom comes to us as Christians when we stop focusing on the _____ in our lives and overcoming it and start looking to our _____ and rejoicing in who He is and what He has accomplished and will continue to accomplish for us!

2. Trusting in ourselves instead of in Christ is evidenced by a lack of _____.
Isaiah 45:21-25
God describes Himself as a _____ God and a _____ (v. 21).
There is _____ God or _____ apart from Him (v. 21).
He invites all people to turn to _____ and be saved (v. 22).
The reason they must turn to Him and be saved is because _____ _____ _____ and _____ _____ _____ _____ (v. 22).
We can find righteousness and strength in the _____ alone. John 15:4 Jesus tells us to remain in _____.
In John 15:4-5 Jesus said we can do nothing apart from Him. In John 15, after telling the disciples that they would produce fruit if they would remain in Him, in verse 11, Jesus said, "I have told you this so that my _____ may be in you and that your _____ may be complete."
Isaiah 45:25 says that all the descendants of Israel will be found _____ and will _____.
In the _____ "all the descendants of Israel will be found righteous and will exult."
Isaiah 44:21-22
God says He has done or will do four things for His children:

1.) "I have _____ you" (v. 21).
2.) "I _____ _____ _____ you" (v. 21).
3.) "I have _____ _____ _____ _____ like a cloud, _____ _____ like the morning mist" (v. 22).
4.) "I have _____ you" (v. 22). He has bought us out of our _____ to _____ and made us His children.

Isaiah is telling the heavens and earth, the mountains, forests, and trees to rejoice because God has _____ Israel (v. 23).
_____ is the result of finding our strength, righteousness, and salvation in the Lord.

3. Trusting in ourselves instead of in Christ is evidenced by a lack of _____.
If you are not experiencing _____, then you are not trusting in God's _____.

Romans 1:7
"To all in Rome who are loved by God and called to be saints: Grace and peace to you from God our Father and from the Lord Jesus Christ."

Galatians 1:3-4
"Grace and peace to you from God our Father and the Lord Jesus Christ, who gave himself for our sins to rescue us from the present evil age."

Revelation 1:4
"Grace and peace to you from him who is, and who was, and who is to come. . ."

Grace and peace come from _____ _____ _____ and the _____ _____ _____.

Romans 15:33
"The God of peace be with you all. Amen."

Romans 16:20
"The God of peace will soon crush Satan under your feet. The grace of our Lord Jesus be with you."

2 Corinthians 13:11
"And the God of love and peace will be with you."

2 Thessalonians 3:16
"Now may the Lord of peace himself give you peace at all times and in every way. The Lord be with all of you."

God is called the God ____ _____. Peace and joy are both listed as fruit of _____ _____ in Galatians 5:22.

Galatians 6:15-16
"Neither circumcision nor uncircumcision means anything; what counts is a new creation. _____ and mercy to all who follow this rule, even to the Israel of God."

_____ and _____ are the result of trusting in the fact that you have been made a new creation by the life of Christ.

Acts 10:36
"You know the message God sent to the people of Israel, telling the good news of _____ through Jesus Christ, who is Lord of all."

Romans 5:1
"Since we have been justified through faith we have _____ with God through our Lord Jesus Christ, through whom we have gained access by faith into this grace in which we now stand. And we rejoice in the hope of the glory of God."

How do both of these verses say that we obtain peace? We have peace with God _____ _____ _____. Because of Christ, we have been given access into _____. We have access into grace by _____. The result of peace with God and standing in grace is _____.
In John 14:27, Jesus said, "_____ I leave with you; my _____ I give you."
What did Christ do in order for us to have peace?
Isaiah 53:5
"But he was pierced for our transgressions, he was crushed for our iniquities; the punishment that brought us peace was upon him, and by his wounds we are healed."
Jesus' punishment brought us _____.
Colossians 1:19-23 tells us how His punishment brought us peace:
"For God was pleased to have all his fullness dwell in him, and through him to reconcile to himself all things, whether things on earth or things in heaven, by _____ _____ through _____ _____, shed on the cross.
"Once you were alienated from God and were enemies in your minds because of your evil behavior. But now he has reconciled you by Christ's physical body through death to present you _____ ____ _____ _____, _____ _____ and _____ _____ _____—if you continue in your faith, established and firm, not moved from the hope held out in the gospel."
Trusting in Christ's righteousness and not our own causes us to say, as is written in Isaiah 26:12: "Lord, you establish _____ for us; _____ that ____ _____ _____ _____ _____ _____ for us."
We have peace as we look to _____ steadfastly to be our righteousness. As Isaiah 26:3 says, "You [God] will keep in perfect peace him whose mind is steadfast, because he _____ in you."
Romans 15:13
"May the God of hope _____ you with _____ _____ and _____ as you _____ in him, so that you may overflow with hope by the power of _____ _____ _____."
It is not that we look to Him to *give* us peace. He Himself *is* our peace!
Ephesians 2:13-14, 17
"But now in Christ Jesus you who once were far away have been brought near through the blood of Christ.
"For ____ _____ ____ _____ _____. . . . He came and preached peace to you who were far away and peace to those who were near."
1 Thessalonians 5:23
"May God himself, the _____ ____ _____, sanctify you through and through. May your whole spirit, soul and body be kept blameless at the coming of our Lord Jesus Christ. The one who calls you is faithful and he will do it."

Who is sanctifying us? The _____ __ _____ is sanctifying us. We have peace because He is doing the work of sanctification for us.

Ephesians 6:14-15

"Stand firm then. . . with your feet fitted with the readiness that comes from the gospel of peace."

We stand firm against Satan because of the _____ we are experiencing as we experience the power of the gospel of _____ at work in us.

Hebrews 13:20-21

"May the God of _____, who through the blood of the eternal covenant brought back from the dead our Lord Jesus, that great Shepherd of the sheep, equip you with everything good for doing his will, and may he work in us what is pleasing to him, through Jesus Christ, to whom be glory for ever and ever. Amen."

Eight

Rooted and Grounded in Love

Not long before we moved back to the United States from Slovakia, I heard a message by Charles Swindoll about David and Mephibosheth. This message was profoundly appropriate to what God had been teaching me about His wonderful grace.

Making It Personal

1. Read 2 Samuel 9:1-13. This story is a beautiful picture of the grace God has offered to us. Notice the kindness offered to Mephibosheth through no merit of his own.

Compare this story to your story found in Ephesians 2:1-9. Can you relate to Mephibosheth? Yes / No

If so, in what ways can you relate to him? _____

_____

2. Read Ephesians 1:2-6. Mephibosheth expected to die because he was Saul's grandson, but instead he was given a place at David's table and ate there "like one of the king's sons" (2 Samuel 9:11).

Describe what we have been given by Christ, also through no merit of our own.
_____
_____

3. Read John 10:28-29. Mephibosheth lived in safety in Jerusalem. As a child of God, where is your place of safety? _____
_____

As I listened to Charles Swindoll expound on this passage, I realized that I, too—undeserving, crippled, and helpless like Mephibosheth—had been given a seat at the table of my King as one of His dear children. There is nothing I can offer Him to make myself more loved and accepted in His sight. He has provided my every need, not because I have earned His favor, but because it was His pleasure to make me His child (Ephesians 1:5). As the words of this beautiful story of God's grace sank deep into my soul, I couldn't hold back the tears. Once again I was captured by His amazing love for me.

Soon after we returned to the United States to live, Bill Elliff, our pastor, preached a series on Romans. God used these messages to profoundly alter my view of God and the grace offered to me in salvation. In that series, Bill made this statement: "At the point of salvation, I became a child of God, and I went from having God as my judge to having God as my Father." Now, I had heard all my life that God was my Father and been taught that I was righteous in His sight because of Christ, but for the first time in my life I realized that the way I viewed God in His relationship toward me was exactly like a judge. He seemed like a judge because I felt that if I didn't do what was right, He was displeased with me. That day I understood that God was my loving heavenly Father who, because of what Christ had done for me, accepted me completely as I was, and there was nothing I could ever do that would cause Him to turn His back on me.

It was as though scales had fallen from my eyes, and now when I read my Bible, I read it in a totally different light. I now plainly see that God's grace, acceptance, and love for His children are everywhere on the pages of Scripture!

Making It Personal

1. Does God seem more to you like your judge or your loving Father? _____

2. Read Romans 5:1-2. We have been justified through _____.

How is it that we have peace with God? _____
_____

In verse 1 the phrase "peace with God" literally means "peace facing God." How would you describe the way you usually feel when you "face God" in prayer?
_____

Who has given us access into grace? _____

3. My pastor explained the phrase "the grace in which we now stand" (v. 2) as meaning that we are now completely wrapped in cords of grace. A similar picture is presented in Psalm 32:10. What does Psalm 32:10 say surrounds the man who trusts in the Lord? _____
_____

Read Psalm 34:7. Who encamps around those who fear the Lord? _____
_____

What does He (see your previous answer) do for those who fear the Lord? _____
_____

(Note: "the angel of the LORD" in the Old Testament refers to Christ.)

When my daughter, Kristina, was young, she would come down every morning and crawl up into my lap and ask if she could cuddle up against me inside my big red robe. I would wrap my robe around her and just sit and snuggle with her for a while. Inside that robe was a place where she found security, love, and complete acceptance. After hearing about being surrounded—or wrapped—in Christ, I began to picture myself crawling up into His lap, like Kristina did into mine, and letting Him pull His big robe of righteousness around me. There I find security, love, and acceptance. I have nothing to prove to Him. I can just be loved.

I have now fallen deeply in love with my Savior because I have developed a keen awareness of what He has done for me. He has not only given me salvation from hell and promised eternal life in heaven, but He sets me free from the sin I face *every day* as I walk the Christian life. Because of what Christ has done, and only by His power, I am able to be set free from sin on a daily basis. When I focus on myself, I see only my inability to do anything good, but when I transfer my focus to Christ, relying only on Him and His power, I find victory. Galatians 3:24 (KJV) says that "the law was our schoolmaster to bring us unto Christ." Knowing the burden of legalism has given me a great appreciation for Christ's power to save me from sin.

> What, then, shall we say in response to this? If God is for us, who can be against us? He who did not spare his own Son, but gave him up for us all—how will he not also, along with him, graciously give us all things? Who will bring any charge against those whom God has chosen? It is God who justifies. Who is he that condemns? Christ Jesus, who died—more than that, who was raised to life—is at the right hand of God and is also interceding for us. [*Wow! Thank God! He doesn't expect perfection. He's interceding for me when I sin.*] Who shall separate us from the love of Christ? Shall trouble or hardship or persecution or famine or nakedness or danger or sword? . . . No, in all these things we are more than conquerors through him who loved us. For I am convinced that neither death nor life, neither angels nor demons, neither the present nor the future, nor any powers, neither height nor depth, nor anything else in all creation [*and that includes my own sin!*], will be able to separate us from the love of God that is in Christ Jesus our Lord. (Romans 8:31-35, 37-39)

Song for Worship and Meditation: "Carried to the Table," sung and written by Leeland, from the album *Sound of Melodies*, 2006

Memory Verse

Who will bring any charge against those whom God has chosen? It is God who justifies. Who is he that condemns? Christ Jesus, who died—more than that, who was raised to life—is at the right hand of God and is also interceding for us. (Romans 8:33-34)

Going Deeper

Suggested Daily Schedule for Week 8

Day 1   Complete Lesson 8.

Day 2   Read Ephesians 3; 1 John 4:11-19; complete pages 180-182.

Day 3   Read Romans 5; complete pages 183-186.

Day 4   Read John 10:1-30; complete pages 187-190.

Day 5   Read Psalm 33; complete pages 191-193.

Viewer Guide
Session 8: Resting in the Love of God

1 John 5:3-5
"This is love for God: to obey His commands. And his commands are not burdensome, for everyone born of God overcomes the world. This is the victory that has overcome the world, even our faith. Who is it that overcomes the world? Only he who believes that Jesus is the Son of God."

John 14:15
"If you love me, you will obey what I command."

Our _____ to the Lord is the evidence that we love Him.

First John 5:3 says God's commands are not _____.

First John 5:3-4 says that God's "commands are not burdensome, for _____ _____ _____ _____ _____ _____ _____."

We overcome the world and its temptations when we understand that the world _____ _____ _____ _____ us, that only God truly satisfies.

It is our _____ that gives us victory over the world and its temptations (vv. 4-5).

Romans 1:5
"Through him and for his name's sake, we received grace and apostleship to call people from among all the Gentiles to the obedience that comes from faith."

Faith results in _____.

How do you grow in your trust and love for a person? You have to _____ ____ _____ that person.

First John 4:19 says that we love God because _____ _____ _____ _____.

1 John 4:8-10

"Whoever does not love does not know God, because God is love. This is how God showed his love among us: He sent his one and only Son into the world that we might live through him. This is love: not that we loved God, but that he loved us and sent his Son as an atoning sacrifice for our sins."

If we do not love God, we do not _____ _____.

1 John 4:16
"And so we know and rely on the love that God has for us. . . . Whoever lives in love lives in God, and God in him."

John 15:9
"As the Father has loved me, so have I loved you. Now remain in my love."

In Psalm 91 when David talks about making "the Most High your dwelling" (v.9), it is clear that he is talking about _____ _____ _____ _____.

Psalm 91:1
"He who dwells in the shelter of the Most High will _____ in the shadow of the Almighty."

Psalm 91:2 "I will say of the Lord, 'He is my _____ and my _____, my God, in whom I _____.'"

Luke 13:34
"O Jerusalem, Jerusalem, you who kill the prophets and stone those sent to you, how often I have longed to gather your children together, as a hen gathers her chicks under her wings, but you were not willing!"

The people of Jerusalem _____ _____ _____ to let Jesus take them under His wings.

Psalm 91:4 says we will find _____ under His wings.
God says He will rescue us if we make Him our dwelling because ____ _____ _____.
In verse 16, what does God say He will show us if we dwell (or rest) in Him? God says if we rest in Him, He will show us His _____.

His Continual Wooing

Always Waiting with Open Arms

Come to me, all you who are weary and burdened, and I will give you rest.

Matthew 11:28

Nine

Running to Christ

There is no formula, no set of instructions to follow to come to a place of rest. Instead, I am learning to let the longings of my soul that once drove me to sin, drive me to a Savior who fills all those longings completely, and I wonder why I would ever choose anything less.

I need to begin this part of my story by saying that I have a wonderful husband. He has been an example of Christ to me and has truly loved me through all the junk that he has had to go through with me—self-righteousness, insecurities, pride, selfish ambitions, self-centeredness . . . It was he who helped me to understand grace by loving me through all this ugliness. We have now had over twenty-five years of a happy, fulfilled marriage. I am madly in love with him.

However, not long after moving back to the States, in spite of having such an unselfish, loving husband, I found myself being drawn to another man. This attraction happened because this man gave me affirmation that Danny had not known how to give, and I realized that I craved that affirmation. (Truth be told, there's no man alive that can meet all the needs of a woman's soul.) When I realized what was happening, I was scared—*very* scared. This man was someone I saw often, and I realized that I could easily fall. I didn't know what to do, so I bought several Christian books about marriage, some written by people who had found themselves in similar situations.

I did not really find the books helpful. But during this time I did the one thing that I had learned to do when struggling previously with selfish ambitions: run to Christ. Whenever the feelings of attraction came, I ran to Christ and allowed Him to meet the longings of my soul. What I actually needed was not a different husband, but to find complete acceptance, affirmation, and love in Christ. As I would run to Him, I found the approval that I so longed for. It was the only way I had strength to overcome the temptation.

What I mean by running to Christ is that I would picture myself in Christ's arms. As I mentally envisioned myself there and experienced His love, approval, and value, I felt so secure that I did not need, or want, to flirt with temptation. There were times when I gave into the temptation to seek this man's approval, but I never made any advances or gave him any indication that I desired a relationship with him. I would also run to Danny. I would go to Danny for intimacy because it helped me to realize that he truly was exactly what I needed and wanted. He was the one whom God, in His sovereignty, had given me; and God, who knows our hearts, knows what is best for us (Jeremiah 29:11). Belief in God's sovereignty in putting us together was definitely key to allowing Christ to overcome this temptation for me.

After a year of dealing with this, I finally told Danny, which I wish I'd done sooner. I had told one other person because I knew I needed to bring it out into the light with someone (see 1 John 1:7-9; James 5:16), but if I had told Danny immediately, he would have fought the temptation with me. The fact that I finally told him was definitely a part of my finding complete victory over it.

Thank God, I did not have to deal with this before I had learned to go to Christ with my selfish ambitions. I had already put into practice running into Christ's arms and resting there in His love when I was dealing with desires for recognition, selfish ambitions, or finding value in my abilities. We fall into sin when we believe Satan's lie that God is not all we need. But running to God for assurance of His love and acceptance of me had made sin lose its power.

Making It Personal

1. Read the following scriptures and fill in the blanks.

Jeremiah 2:13

My people have committed two sins: They have forsaken ____, the spring of _____ _____, and have dug their own cisterns, _____ cisterns that cannot hold water.

John 4:10

Jesus answered her, "If you knew the gift of God and who it is that asks you for a drink, you would have asked _____ and ____ would have given you _____ _____."

Isaiah 55:1-3

Come, all you who are _____, come to the waters; and you who have _____ _____, come, buy and eat! Come, buy wine and milk without money and _____ _____. Why spend money on what is not bread, and your labor on what does not _____? Listen, listen to me, and eat what is good, and your _____ will _____ in the richest of fare. Give ear and come to ____; hear_____, that your _____ may live.

2. Read Ephesians 6:10-18.

What is the first piece of armor that we are to put on (v. 14)?
_____

According to John 14:6, who is the truth? _____

What is the second piece of armor (v. 14)? _____

According to 1 Corinthians 1:30, who is our righteousness? _____

What is the third piece of armor (v. 15)? _____

According to Ephesians 2:13-14, who is our peace? _____

What is the fourth piece of armor (v. 16)? _____

According to Hebrews 12:2, who is the "author and perfecter of our faith"? _____

What is the fifth piece of armor (v. 17)? _____

According to Psalm 62:1-2, who is our salvation? _____

What is the sixth piece of armor (v. 17)? _____

According to John 1:1 and Revelation 19:11-13, who is the Word of God? _____

3. Read Romans 13:14. To put on the armor means to put on _____.

4. Read Psalm 3:3 and fill in the blanks.

    But _____ are a _____ around me, O _____; _____ bestow _____ on me and _____ up my head.

It is impossible to float on water if we struggle. In order to stay above water, a person must completely relax and allow the water to hold him up. In the same way, we must stop striving to save ourselves and allow Christ, the One who has already done all the work for us, to hold us up. All we must do is simply rest in His arms.

I have learned that I cannot focus on how good or bad I am. I have learned instead to take my eyes off myself and put them on Christ. My soul has been flooded with joy and peace as He has taken me into His arms and loved me. He has pulled me into His lap and nestled me close to Him as He put His big robe of righteousness around me; and as long as I am staying close to His heart and hearing His heart beat with love for me, I do not struggle so much with sin. When I am dealing with temptation of any kind, all I have to do is run back into His arms and rest in who I am as His child and get all my needs met in Him, and He breaks the power of that sin over me.

The following entries to my journal summarize the reason I have written this Bible study.

January 11, 2008

I woke up this morning feeling very at peace and in love with the Lord. I realized I had not felt this way in a long time. I realized that I had not felt God's approval of me because my sin was in the way (so I thought) and had felt that God was against me. I'm beginning to see that this has been a struggle all my life—instead of running to God when I'm struggling with sin, I feel like God is displeased with me for struggling and so I try to deal with the sin on my own. Though I'm calling out for Him to help me overcome the sin, I have this feeling that He is displeased with me because of my sinful heart—which drives me to seek the approval of man.

I find myself looking for recognition and approval from men because I'm insecure in my relationship with God. Then I feel guilt over selfish ambitions which raise their ugly heads again because of this lack of security in God's approval, and it is a vicious cycle. This all happens because I've believed (and for most of my life I've believed) one huge lie that God is against me when I sin. This is not true because, as a Christian, I am totally accepted in God's sight because of what Christ did for me on the cross! "He forgave us all our sins, having canceled the written code, with its regulations, that was against us and that stood opposed to us; he took it away, nailing it to the cross" (Colossians 2:13-14). He sees me clothed with Christ's righteousness. "Therefore, brothers, since we have confidence to enter the Most Holy Place by the blood of Jesus, by a new and living way opened for us through the curtain, that is, his body, and since we have a great priest over the house of God, let us draw near to God with a sincere heart in full assurance of faith, having our hearts sprinkled to cleanse us from a guilty conscience and having our bodies washed with pure water" (Hebrews 10:19-22). Jesus said, "You are already clean because of the word I have spoken to you" (John 15:3). "Let us therefore come boldly unto the throne <u>of grace</u>, that we may obtain mercy, and find <u>grace</u> to help in time of need" (Hebrews 4:16 KJV).

Oh God, thank you for your great love and for setting me free from myself! Thank you that as your child and because of what Christ has done for me, You are never against me! My heart rejoices, and I feel like singing and shouting!

April 7, 2008

Dear Savior,

I've traveled so much of this journey alone. I'm tired of trying to make it on my own. Every time I get a glimpse of You or fall into Your arms for comfort or from exhaustion, I find such joy, such peace, such rest. But somehow I don't stay there, I find myself in the arms of another—the arms of ambition, of selfishness, of in submission. In recent years, the path has become steep, up mountainous terrain with sharp cutting rocks, and I have found myself in Your arms more often because I've known I could not make it alone. I am beginning to understand who You are because of these difficult paths. Your great love and compassion have captivated me. Your willingness to fight for me on many occasions when the lion came to devour me has made me feel passionately in love with You. Yet when the path has smoothed out and the enemy seems far away, I let You know that I'm sure I can make it alone, and so I force You away. My love wanes, and I tell you that I would rather have someone else or some other thing bring me the happiness or comfort that I need on my journey. And then I stumble again because what appeared to be mere cobblestones ahead have turned into huge rocks obstructing my path — rocks that I can never climb without Your help.

Yet even when there are no obstacles that I can't overcome, I simply find myself despairing because of the lack of Your wonderful presence. When you are not near, I have begun to long, not for Your help, but for <u>You</u>. I have felt Your strong arms around me and heard Your tender words of love. I have been enraptured by Your beautiful face. And I know that no one or no thing can delight my soul and give me the happiness that You give.

Today, I heard You calling down to me, "My dove in the clefts of the rock, in the hiding places on the mountainside, show me your face, let me hear your voice; for your voice is sweet, and your face is lovely."[5] I saw You on the precipice above me with Your hand reaching down to mine saying, "Come away with me, my bride. Arise, my darling, my beautiful one, and come with me. See! The winter is past; the rains are over and gone. Flowers appear on the earth; the season of singing has come, the cooing of doves is heard in our land. The fig tree forms its early fruit; the blossoming vines spread their fragrance. Arise, come, my darling; my beautiful one, come with me.[6] The view is awesome up here."

I know now that what You say is true. For though the path at times has been dangerously jagged and steep, You have always led me into green pastures and beside quiet waters. The words that You have spoken to me have brought restoration like water to my thirsty soul. <u>You</u> and You alone are what I truly long for. So today when I heard your voice, I looked up at Your beauty, and I wondered how my heart could ever have been drawn away. Why am I so prone to wander from my heart's one true Desire? I determined it must never happen again and called out to You to please, <u>always</u> keep me close by Your side and to never ever let me leave You again. You reached down and grabbed my hand. I said, "Take me away with you — let us hurry! Let the king bring me into his chambers.[7] Let Him kiss me with the kisses of His mouth — for Your love is more delightful than wine.[8] Come away, my lover, and be like a gazelle or like a young stag on the spice-laden mountains.[9] Place me like a seal over your heart, like a seal on your arm; for love is as strong as death, its jealousy unyielding as the grave. It burns like blazing fire, like a mighty flame. Many waters cannot quench love; rivers cannot wash it away.[10] I am forever Yours and Yours alone." "I belong to my lover, and his desire is for me."[11]

With all my love,
Your Princess

Song for Worship and Meditation: "My Beloved" sung and written by Kari Jobe, from album *Kari Jobe*, 2009

Memory Verse

The LORD appeared to us in the past, saying: "I have loved you with an everlasting love; I have drawn you with loving-kindness." (Jeremiah 31:3)

Going Deeper

Suggested Daily Schedule for Week 9

Day 1   Complete Lesson 9.

Day 2   Read John 4:1-42; complete pages 194-197.

Day 3   Read Song of Songs 1; complete pages 198-200.

Day 4   Read Songs of Songs 2:1-7; complete pages 201-203.

Day 5   Read Song of Songs 2:8-16; 4:7-16; complete pages 204-207.

Viewer Guide
Session 9: Finding Satisfaction in God

Ephesians 3:16-19

Paul is praying here for the Ephesians not that *they* would abide in *Christ*, but that _____ would dwell _____ _____ through faith. We know he is writing to believers because he calls them saints in Ephesians 1:1, 18. Jesus also said to His disciples in John 15:4, "Remain in me, and _____ _____ _____ _____ _____." In John 14:23, Jesus said, "If anyone loves me, he will obey my teaching. My Father will love him, and _____ _____ come to him and _____ _____ _____ _____ _____." So we can see from these verses that as believers, not only do we abide in God when we in trust take refuge in Him, but the result of that same faith in Him is that He abides in us! Notice that Christ dwelling in our hearts is a work of the _____ that He accomplishes because of our _____. (It is as we are strengthened with power through the Spirit of God in our inner being [v. 16] that Christ dwells in our hearts through faith [v. 17].) We know from Colossians 1:19 that all the fullness of God dwells in Christ and so when Christ dwells in our hearts, amazingly, the _____ _____ _____ lives in us!

Paul said that _____ the _____ _____ _____ would cause the Ephesians to be filled to the measure with all the fullness of God (v. 19). Here we see that when we get to know the love Christ has for us, we are filled completely with the fullness of God. I like to think of this as _____ _____ _____ _____ _____ _____ _____ _____ of unmet needs in my life. Proverbs 19:22 says that "what a man desires is unfailing love." If this is what my soul desires, and God is love (1 John 4:16), then what my soul desires is _____ _____.

Psalm 63

When David says, "O God, you are my God," he is expressing to God that He _____ is his God. He is not looking to anyone or anything else to be his _____.

He was _____ seeking God.

This desert of Judah that David was in must have reminded him of his spiritual thirst because this psalm is a prayer expressing David's _____ for God. He describes the place in which he is as one with no _____ (v. 1). Not only is he in a place physically where he could find no water, but David was also in a place spiritually where he could find _____ to _____ _____ _____.

Psalm 63:2 makes it clear that in the house of the Lord, David had gotten a glimpse of _____ and His power and glory. Because of what Christ has done for us, you and I have the privilege of _____ His temple, and Jesus' invitation to us is to abide in Him and allow Him to abide in us continually!

David wanted to glorify God as long as he lived because he had discovered that _____ _____ was _____ _____ _____ (vv. 3-4).

David knew satisfaction for his soul was in the _____ ____ _____ (vv. 3-5).

David found himself thinking about _____ and His goodness all throughout the night (v. 6).

Psalm 63:5; 34:8; 36:7-8

When we get a taste of Him, we experience His _____ _____ and _____.

David responded to God's help by _____ (v. 7).

He sang in the _____ ____ _____ _____ (v. 7).

Psalm 57:1, David prayed, "Have mercy on me, O God, have mercy on me, for in you my soul takes refuge. I will take refuge in the shadow of your wings until the disaster has passed."

David experienced being in the shadow of God's wings because he had _____ _____ _____ _____.

Psalm 18:30, 35

"He is a _____ for all who take refuge in him. You give me your shield of victory, and your _____ _____ _____ _____; you stoop down to make me great." Psalm 63:8 says that _____ _____ _____ _____ _____ and verses 9-10 describe him being a _____ of protection for us.

Saul and his men were seeking David to _____ him (vv. 9-10).

1 Samuel 23:15, 16

"While David was at Horesh in the Desert of Ziph, he learned that Saul had come out to take his life. And Saul's son Jonathan went to David at Horesh and helped him find strength in God. 'Don't be afraid,' he said. 'My father Saul will not lay a hand on you. You will be king over Israel, and I will be second to you. Even my father Saul knows this.'"

David was confident of God's help because of his faith in _____ _____.

David said, "They who seek my life will be destroyed (Psalm 63:9), . . . but the king will rejoice in God (v. 11)." David was trusting in God's promise that he would become king, and his response to the refuge and satisfaction he found in God was _____ ____ _____ _____ and _____ to Him (v. 11).

*Though the fig tree does not bud
and there are no grapes on the vines,
though the olive crop fails
and the fields produce no food,
though there are no sheep in the pen
and no cattle in the stalls,
yet I will rejoice in the L*ORD*,
I will be joyful in God my Savior.
The Sovereign L*ORD *is my strength;
he makes my feet like the feet of a deer,
he enables me to go on the heights.*

HABAKKUK 3:17-19

Going Deeper

I am providing these "Going Deeper" questions to prompt you to think about the specific areas that are dealt with in each lesson. The scriptures I've listed are those God used to teach me the things I have shared in *Loved*.

Each day, before you read and answer the questions, ask God to open your eyes so that you may see the truth in His word that you personally need to be set free.

Week 1
Day 2: Romans 6

Read Romans 6.

Before exploring the truths of this chapter that address our battle with sin, it is important to understand that Romans 6:3-4 is not talking about a physical water baptism, rather it speaks of our being identified with Christ in His death and resurrection (Romans 6:5). According to *Strong's Exhaustive Concordance*,[12] the word "baptized" in verse 3 literally means "*to make whelmed* (i.e. *fully wet*)." To establish the meaning of the word "baptized" in Romans 6, take a look at how this same Greek word (and noun in verse 4) are used in the following passages:

> When they [the Pharisees] come from the marketplace they do not eat unless they wash [baptize]. And they observe many other traditions, such as the washing [baptismos] of cups, pitchers and kettles. (Mark 7:4)

> But the Pharisee, noticing that Jesus did not first wash [baptize] before the meal, was surprised. (Luke 11:38)

> For I do not want you to be ignorant of the fact, brothers, that our forefathers were all under the cloud and that they all passed through the sea. They were all baptized into Moses in the cloud and in the sea. (1 Corinthians 10:1-2)

In the first two passages, it is clear that the word baptize means "to wash." In the last passage, the word "baptized" cannot mean "washed" or a literal immersion into water at all because the cloud went before the Israelites to guide them on their way, and they did not get wet by the sea but passed through the sea on dry ground. From this passage, we can deduce that the word "baptized" means brought into a covenant relationship with Moses. It speaks of the Israelites being identified with Moses and his leadership, and ultimately under God's protection and leadership.

Romans 6:3 could be stated as follows: "Or don't you know that all of us who were completely immersed into Christ Jesus were completely immersed into his death?" Scripture makes it clear over and over that it is faith in Christ's sacrificial death for us and His resurrection from the dead that saves us from sin and places us in right standing with God (e.g., Romans 4:24-5:2), not any physical act; therefore, we know that water baptism cannot save our souls. Rather, water baptism is merely a picture of our death and resurrection with Christ, symbolizing the washing away of our sins by His blood and our complete immersion into Him in a covenant relationship.

1. What question is raised in Romans 6:1?

2. Verses 2-7 say that we died to sin. Read these verses again as well as Galatians 2:20; 5:24; and 1 Peter 2:24. Explain what you think it means to have "died to sin."

Christ died in our place. When He died, He took our sins upon Himself and paid the penalty for them (1 Peter 2:24). Not only that, but when He died on the cross, our "old self" was crucified with Him (Romans 6:6). This means that because our old master is dead, we are no longer enslaved to our sinful nature.

3. According to verse 4, we died with Christ for what purpose?

4. According to Galatians 2:20, how are we to live our new life?

5. According to verse 6, why was "our old self" crucified?

6. From what have we been set free (v. 7)?

7. If we died with Christ, is it necessary that we die to sin over and over again (vv. 8-10)?

8. According to verses 4-5 and verses 8-10, what significance does being united with Christ in His resurrection from the dead have on our spiritual lives?

Verse 4 says that Christ was raised from the dead so that we, too, may live a new life! We not only died to sin, but we have been raised with Christ and become spiritually born again to live for God (v. 10).

9. In the same way that Christ died but now lives, what should we consider to be true about ourselves (v. 11)?

10. According to verse 12, if we are dead to sin and alive to God, what relationship do we now have with sin?

11. Who should we surrender ourselves to instead (v. 13)?

We died with Christ to sin, which means sin's power in us was broken on the cross. However, verse 11 says that we must count on the fact that this is true. If we do not, even as Christians we can live as though sin were still our master. If it were impossible for us to allow sin to rule over us, then we would not be admonished to consider ourselves dead and to yield our bodies to God as those who have been brought back from the dead.

Read Colossians 3:1-5.

12. Since we died with Christ (Colossians 3:3) and have been raised with Christ (Colossians 3:1), what does Colossians 3:5 tell us to do?

13. Meditate on Romans 6:14. Grace can be defined as "receiving what one does not deserve." How does God's grace keep a person from being mastered by sin?

It is grace that enables us not to sin. When we realize we are incapable of doing anything good, if we will only look to Him for help, He will do for us what we cannot do ourselves.

14. Why is it not logical to conclude that because God is gracious, we can sin all we want (vv. 15-16)?

15. Verse 16 teaches us that we have only two masters to choose from. What are these two masters, and what is the result of yielding to each one?

16. Paul said that those to whom he was writing had "obeyed the form of teaching to which [they had been] entrusted" (v. 17). According to Romans 1:5, 8, what had caused them to obey?

17. According to Romans 6:18, what did their faith in Christ do for them?

18. According to verse 19, what should we now offer our bodies to?

19. Being a slave to sin keeps us free from what (v. 20)?

20. In order to keep us from surrendering to God, Satan tries to make us believe we will benefit from sinning. In verse 21, Paul attacks this lie with the truth. What did Paul say we actually reap from our sin?

21. With this in mind, if you are not desperate to turn from sin in your life, what lie have you believed?

22. If we have been set free from sin by the death of Christ, who have we become slaves to (v. 22)?

23. What benefit do we reap from yielding ourselves as slaves to God (v. 22)?

24. What is the result of Christ producing holiness in us (v. 22)?

25. Romans 6:23 is often cited to help people who do not know Christ see that the penalty of their sin is death but that God offers them life in Christ. Of course, it is true that sin brings death and that God offers to everyone life in Jesus, but Paul actually wrote this as a warning to *believers* about the effects of sin. Read Proverbs 11:18 and Proverbs 14:12, and then list some of the ways that sin has brought death to you.

26. What free gift does God offer to you as a believer in Christ Jesus (Romans 6:23)?

27. This means that you don't have to continue to live in the death that your sin has been producing in you! Look back to question 18. What is the only thing required of you as a Christian in order to experience freedom from sin and reap the benefit of life?

28. Look back over the questions and answers for today's scripture reading, and highlight any truths that are new to you or that you have not been believing. Write or verbalize a prayer to God, confessing any sin that is still producing death in you and asking Him to give you the faith to believe that sin is no longer your master.

Week 1
Day 3: Romans 7

Read Romans 7.

1. We not only died to sin (Romans 6), but according to Romans 7:4, what else did we die to?

2. According to the analogy used in verses 1-3, what does being dead to the law mean for us?

Because we have died to the law, the law is no longer our authority. It is not what we are to be serving.

3. For what purpose did we who have placed our faith in Christ die to the law (v. 4)?

4. What is the result of our union with Christ (v. 4)?

5. According to verses 5 and 8, when our sinful natures were our masters, did the law help us in any way to do what was right? Yes / No

What did the law actually do for us (v. 5)?

6. What have we been set free to do (v. 6)?

7. What was the purpose of the law (v. 7)?

8. According to verses 8-11, did the law bring death or life?

9. Since the law causes death in us, can we conclude that the law is bad (v. 12)? Yes / No

Why, or why not (v. 13)?

10. Describe the struggle that Paul talks about in verses 14-25.

11. According to verses 14-25, why do we struggle with doing what is good?

12. Why are we unable to do the good we want to do (vv. 14-15)?

God allows us to try in our own strength to battle with sin until we come to the realization that we are incapable of overcoming it. This is true whether you are a believer or not. If a Christian begins to think that she can produce righteousness on her own, or contribute to it at all, she will be powerless to overcome sin. Though she has the power of God within her, she will not be able to appropriate it.

13. Besides God's law (which Paul said he was a slave to), what other law did he see at work waging war against him (vv. 21-25)?

14. Our sinful nature wages war against our inner being, which delights in God's law. Where does victory lie (v. 25)?

15. What is your only hope for deliverance from the law of sin and its power over your life (v. 25)?

16. Spend some time thanking God for delivering you from your slavery to sin.

Week 1
Day 4: Romans 8:1-16

Read Romans 8:1-16.

1. What keeps us from being condemned for the sin that we continually deal with (vv. 1-3)?

2. Why are we who are in Christ not condemned (vv. 1-3)?

If we belong to Christ, He does not condemn us when we sin. He does not look on us with displeasure, waiting for us to get our act together and become righteous, because He knows that we are *incapable* of overcoming sin. But this does not mean that God overlooks our sin; through Christ, He has delivered us from its power. Rather than condemning us, "through Christ Jesus the law of the Spirit of life set [us] free from the law of sin and death." This means that God has already accomplished for us what we cannot do for ourselves.

3. Though *we* are not condemned, what *has* God condemned (v. 3)?

4. How did God condemn (or punish) our sin (v. 3)?

God condemned our sin by sending Jesus to take the punishment for it.

5. What is the only way for us to meet the righteous requirements of the law (v. 4)?

6. What causes us to have our minds set on what the Spirit desires (v. 5, Galatians 5:16)?

7. What is the result of living according to the sinful nature (or in other words, just doing whatever comes naturally to us as humans) (vv. 6, 13)?

8. What is the result of having our minds controlled by the Spirit of God (v. 6)?

9. According to verses 7-8, to what degree are we able to obey God's law or please God apart from the Spirit of God controlling us?

10. If you belong to Christ, who is now your master (v. 9)?

11. Who has the Spirit of Christ living inside of them (v. 9)?

12. What is true about those who have Christ living inside of them (v. 10)?

13. Compare verses 10-11 to Romans 6:5-10. Who or what has died in each of these passages?

Who or what is now alive according to these passages?

The same power that raised Christ from the dead is at work in us to give spiritual life to our mortal bodies and make them capable of producing spiritual fruit.

I pray also that the eyes of your heart may be enlightened in order that you may know . . . his incomparably great power for us who believe. That power is like the working of his mighty strength, which he exerted in Christ when he raised him from the dead and seated him at his right hand in the heavenly realms. (Ephesians 1:18-20)

14. Do you live as though this mighty power is at your disposal?

15. What is the only way for us to put sin to death (v. 13)?

16. If you allow the Spirit to lead you, what does this say about you (v. 14)?

17. Why do we not have to be afraid of God (vv. 15-16)?

18. What do you suppose is meant by "again" in verse 15?

19. According to 1 John 4:17-18, what causes fear?

Trying to keep the law makes a person afraid because if he is honest with himself, he knows he is failing miserably to live up to God's righteous standards and will be judged and punished.

20. What fears are you experiencing?

21. Romans 8:15-16 assures us that we are no longer fearful slaves but are now children of God. Read 1 John 3:1 and 4:19. When we know the love that the Father has for us, what takes the place of fear in motivating us to obey Him?

22. Meditate on what you learned today about yourself. If you are in Christ Jesus,

    - there is no condemnation for you,
    - you are not controlled by the sinful nature but by the Spirit,
    - you are not a slave who must serve God out of fear, and
    - you are a beloved child of God.

Write out your response to God, thanking Him for these wonderful truths.

Week 1
Day 5: 2 Corinthians 12:1-10; Matthew 9:10-13; Luke 14:15-24; 2 Corinthians 10:12, 17-18; 1 Corinthians 1:17-31

Read 2 Corinthians 12:1-10.

1. What did Paul say he would gladly boast about (v. 9)?

Why?

2. How did Paul feel about his weaknesses and difficulties (v. 10)?

Why?

Read Matthew 9:10-13

3. Who desired to spend time with the needy (vv. 11-12)?

Why?

4. Ponder what Jesus meant by "I desire mercy, not sacrifice." He told the Pharisees to learn what this means (v. 13). For insight into its meaning, read Hosea 6:6; Micah 6:8; and Psalm 51:16-17. Write down what you think the Lord meant by this statement.

5. What is wonderful about seeing our sinfulness and neediness (v. 13)?

6. Were the tax collectors and "sinners" truly more sinful than the Pharisees (Romans 7:18)?

Read Luke 14:15-24.

7. What is this great banquet a picture of? (see Isaiah 55:1-3; Revelation 19:9)

8. Why do you think those who were first invited to the banquet refused to come?

9. Who did the master end up having for guests at his banquet (v. 21)?

10. Matthew Henry's *Concise Commentary* explains this parable as follows:

> In this parable observe the free grace and mercy of God shining in the gospel of Christ, which will be food and a feast for the soul of a man that knows its own wants and miseries. All found some pretence to put off their attendance. This reproves the Jewish nation for their neglect of the offers of Christ's grace … The want of gratitude in those who slight gospel offers, and the contempt put upon the God of heaven thereby, justly provoke him. The apostles were to turn to the Gentiles, when the Jews refused the offer; and with them the church was filled. The provision made for precious souls in the gospel of Christ, has not been made in vain; for if some reject, others will thankfully accept the offer. The very poor and low in the world, shall be as welcome to Christ as the rich and great; and many times the gospel has the greatest success among those that labour under worldly disadvantages and bodily infirmities.[13]

Why do you think the gospel is more readily received by those who are "very poor and low in the world" or with "worldly disadvantages and bodily infirmities" than those who are less needy?

Read 2 Corinthians 10:12, 17-18.

11. According to 2 Corinthians 10:12, why should we not compare ourselves with others?

12. Why is it an affront to God to boast about ourselves and our accomplishments (Isaiah 42:8; 48:11)?

13. In what ways are we not being truthful when we do so (1 Corinthians 4:7)?

14. Who did Paul say is the only one we should boast in (2 Corinthians 10:17)?

15. Why did Paul say he would boast about the things that showed his weakness (2 Corinthians 11:30; 12:5, 9-10)?

Read 1 Corinthians 1:17-31.

16. Why does God choose foolish and weak people (vv. 27-29; Matthew 9:10-13; Luke 14:15-24)?

17. List what Christ has become for you and what that means (1 Corinthians 1:30), and spend some time praising Him for this.

18. About whom or what will you choose to boast today?

Week 2
Day 2: Romans 12:1-2; Ephesians 4:22-24; Colossians 3:9-10; Romans 13:12-14

Read Romans 12:1-2.
1. Which of the following are we told to consider in offering our bodies as living sacrifices to God? (Choose only one.)

    a. God's justice
    b. God's power
    c. God's mercy

Why do you think this is so?

What effect does trusting in God's mercy have on your offering yourself to Him as a living sacrifice?

2. Offering ourselves as living sacrifices means surrendering our lives in complete trust to the Father. The reason we have difficulty surrendering ourselves to Him is because we are not certain that He can be trusted. What does Hebrews 4:16 say we will receive if we approach the throne of God with confidence?
Do you think this includes approaching the throne of God to offer yourself as a living sacrifice?

3. According to Romans 12:2, how can we keep from being conformed to the culture of the world?

4. List some areas in which your mind needs to be renewed.

5. What is the result of having our minds renewed (v. 2)?

Read Ephesians 4:22-24.

6. These verses say that the Ephesians were taught to do three things. The first thing listed that they had been taught was to put something off. What was that (v. 22)?

7. What causes the old self to self-destruct (v. 22)?

8. How have the desires of your sinful nature (the old self) deceived you (v. 22)?

This is important for us to understand. The desires of our old nature are deceitful in that we think they will bring satisfaction and fulfillment to us, but they will actually destroy us. (Remember Romans 6:21.)

9. Read 2 Peter 2:18-19. It is easy to become enticed, even as Christians, into looking somewhere other than Christ to have the needs of our souls met. What are you tempted to seek for satisfaction and freedom that, when given into, actually enslaves you?

10. What was the second thing the Ephesians had been taught (v. 23)?

11. How can we "be made new in the attitude of our minds" or, as Romans 12:2 says, "renew our minds"?

The Word of God is the key to renewing our minds. The more we know and understand the Word of God, the more we will think the way God thinks and the deceitfulness of sin will become apparent to us. (Hebrew 4:12)

12. What was the third thing the Ephesians had been taught? (Ephesians 4:24)

13. Describe what this "new self" was created to be like (v. 24).

Read Colossians 3:9-10.

14. According to Colossians 3:10, how is our new self renewed in the image of God?

Colossians 3:10 teaches that we are made new—in the image of our Creator—as we grow in our knowledge of Him. So in order to be *like* God, we must get to *know* God. With this in mind, we can conclude from this verse and Romans 12:2 that we are transformed into His likeness as we renew our minds about who He is and what He is like.
    Read Romans 13:12-14.

15. What does verse 14 tell us to put on (or clothe ourselves with)? (see also Galatians 2:20)

16. According to Colossians 3:12, how are we to clothe ourselves?

Christ is our righteousness (1 Corinthians 1:30; Philippians 3:9). Whenever Scripture talks about clothing ourselves with righteousness, it is talking about covering ourselves in the righteousness of Christ, fully trusting in His righteousness and not our own. We have a beautiful picture of this in Genesis 3:21.

After Adam and Eve sinned, God killed an animal to make garments of skin to clothe them and cover their nakedness and shame. In the same way, Christ died for us in order to cover our nakedness and shame with His righteousness. Envision yourself completely wrapped with the righteousness of Christ, your shame no longer exposed, standing before the Father without fault and free from the fear of condemnation. Spend some time thanking Him for the joy and freedom this brings.

Week 2
Day 3: Galatians 5:16-26

Read Galatians 5:16-26.

1. According to verse 16, how can you keep from giving in to the desires of the sinful nature?

2. The conflict between the Spirit and man's sinful nature, described in verse 17, is also described in Romans 7:14-21. Since we are incapable of doing the good that we want to do, what is our only hope, according to Galatians 5:16 and Romans 8:4?

3. Describe what it means to be led by someone.

With this is mind, what do you think it means to be "led by the Spirit" (v. 18)?

4. If the Spirit is the one guiding and directing us, what do we not have to worry about (v. 18)?

We do not have to be concerned about trying to please God by keeping the law. In fact, Romans 6:14 teaches that sin was our master when we were under the law. The Spirit, not the law or any other code of regulations, has the power to make us righteous.

5. Look at the list of sins that our sinful natures produce (vv. 17-21). What happens to those who live like this (v. 21)? (This word *live* means to do repetitiously.)

6. Now look at the list of the fruit the Spirit produces (vv. 22-23). According to Galatians 6:8 and Romans 8:6, what do you gain if the fruit of the Spirit is being produced in your life?

Are you experiencing the life and peace that come from being controlled by the Spirit?

7. What does Galatians 5:24 say that those who belong to Christ have done?

According to Romans 6:6, with whom was our sinful nature (old self) crucified?

Why? (Romans 6:7)

8. Galatians 5:25 says that we not only live by the Spirit, but we are also to walk by the Spirit. The Greek word translated *live* in verse 16 actually means *to walk*. The word translated *keep in step* in verse 25 describes more specifically how we are to walk with the Spirit. The word translated *live* in verse 25 can only be translated *live*. Therefore, verse 25 could be paraphrased as follows: "Since the Spirit has given us spiritual life, let's live our lives in step with Him." In light of this, what is the answer to Paul's question in Galatians 3:2?

If we received the Spirit by faith, then how are we to "keep in step with the Spirit" (Galatians 3:3)?

9. What keeps us from experiencing the fruit of the Spirit and causes us to provoke and envy one another (Galatians 5:26)?

10. According to this passage, which of the following should you seek after in order to have the fruit of the Spirit produced in your life?

    a. love, joy, peace, patience, kindness, goodness, faithfulness, gentleness, self-control
    b. the Spirit of God Himself

It is humanly impossible to produce the fruit of the Spirit. Therefore, it is not good character that we should try to obtain; rather, as we look to Christ and trust His finished work for us, the Spirit of Christ produces godly character in us.

11. Think about how you have been attempting to live the Christian life. Have you been looking to the Lord to live out His righteousness through you, or have you been trying in your own effort to please Him?

When we attempt to live righteously apart from dependence on the Spirit of God, it is because we think we are really capable of doing so. Is the Lord pointing out any areas of pride in your life? Humble yourself before Him, asking Him to help you to know how to consistently walk in the Spirit.

Week 2
Day 4: John 7:37-39; 1 Corinthians 12:12-13; Ephesians 5:18-21; Colossians 3:14-18

Read John 7:37-39.

1. According to verse 37, where do we find drink for our thirsty souls (satisfaction for our deepest longings)?

2. What do we need to do in order to have living water flow from within us (v. 38)?

3. In verse 39, what did Jesus say the "living water" was that would flow from the person who believes in Him?

Read 1 Corinthians 12:12-13.

4. How many of those in the body of Christ were given the Spirit to drink (v. 13)?

Read Ephesians 5:18-21.

5. Why do you suppose Paul (the author of Ephesians) contrasts being filled with the Spirit to being drunk with wine?

6. How does a person get drunk with wine?

7. In John 7:37, whom did Jesus say we should go to for drink when we are thirsty?

8. Jesus said that living water (the Holy Spirit) flows from within believers. How then, can we practically be filled with the Spirit?

   In the same way that wine can control us, being filled with the Spirit means that we have drunk deeply of the living water of the Spirit until we are filled with Him and controlled by Him.

   All of us who are believers in Christ already have the Spirit of God living in us (John 7:38; 1 Corinthians 12:13; Romans 8:9), but Ephesians 5:18 commands us to "be filled with the Spirit." This phrase in the Greek means "keep on being filled," or in other words, "keep on allowing the Spirit to fill you."

   How can we do this? Read Ephesians 5:18-21 in the King James Version:

And be not drunk with wine, wherein is excess; but be filled with the Spirit; speaking to yourselves in psalms and hymns and spiritual songs, singing and making melody in your heart to the Lord; giving thanks always for all things unto God and the Father in the name of our Lord Jesus Christ; submitting yourselves one to another in the fear of God.

What are the four things we are encouraged to do in conjunction with being filled with the Spirit? (Fill in the following blanks.)

1.) _____ to _____ in psalms and hymns and spiritual songs,
2.) _____ and making melody in _____ _____ to the Lord.
3.) _____ _____ _____ for _____ things unto God and the Father in the name of our Lord Jesus Christ,
4.) _____ yourselves _____ ____ _____ in the fear of God."

9. Read Colossians 3:14-18 and write down the things that you find in these verses that are similar to the things you listed above from Ephesians 5:18-21:

   1.)

   2.)

   3.)

   4.)

10. We can conclude that drinking deeply of the Spirit of God and being filled with Him involves the following:

    1.) Speaking the truth of God's Word to ourselves and to others
    2.) Singing or listening to worship music that lifts our thoughts from ourselves and our problems to God and who He is
    3.) Continually giving thanks to God for who He is and what He has done for us
    4.) Submitting to others out of reverence and appreciation for Christ

Will you drink deeply of Him today, allowing Him to fill every nook and cranny of your inner being? He alone can satisfy your soul.

Week 2
Day 5: Philippians 3

Read Philippians 3.

1. Where is joy found (v. 1)?

2. Who is Paul referring to as the "dogs, those men who do evil, those mutilators of the flesh" in verse 2 (see also Galatians 5:2-6)?

Paul is referring to those who insist that a man must be circumcised to be right with God. They are doing evil because they are trusting in their own works to justify them rather than in Christ.

3. If we are not finding joy in the Lord as our righteousness (v. 1), what does this indicate that we are putting our confidence in and looking to for salvation (v. 3)?

4. In verse 3, how much confidence did Paul say he put in the "flesh" (human or sinful nature)?

5. How do we who are the truly circumcised worship (v. 3)? (For an explanation of what true circumcision is, see Colossians 2:11.)

6. Who do we glory in (v. 3)?

7. Is Christ the one you are placing your confidence in, or do you find yourself feeling spiritually proud or inferior to others? (Both pride and inferiority are indications you are putting confidence in the flesh.)

8. Look at Paul's accomplishments in verses 4-6. What are the ways in which you have put confidence in yourself to gain acceptance or approval from God?

9. What did Paul learn was of far greater value than all his "qualifications" (vv. 7-10)?

10. Knowing Christ was of such great value to Paul that he was willing to lose everything else to gain Him. Have you found this same great treasure in the person of Christ?

If not, what are you trusting in to make you righteous that is keeping you from experiencing the righteousness of Christ?

Or what are you trusting in to bring you joy and fulfillment that is keeping you from experiencing joy and fulfillment in Christ?

11. Do you consider all your accomplishments as totally worthless in order to gain Christ and His righteousness?

12. How do we gain the righteousness of Christ (v. 9)?

13. What three things does Paul state in verse 10 that he wants to know?

Paul wanted to know Christ, the fellowship of His sufferings, and the power of His resurrection.

14. We can know "the power of [Christ's] resurrection and the fellowship of sharing in his sufferings" both spiritually and physically. We became like Christ in his death, spiritually speaking, when we were crucified with Christ (Galatians 2:20; Romans 6:2-8). And we have experienced the power of Christ's resurrection by being made spiritually alive (Ephesians 2:4-5; Romans 6:4). In order to understand how we may physically share in Christ's sufferings, read 1 Peter 4:12-14. When we participate in Christ's sufferings by suffering as His followers, what does 1 Peter 4:14 say rests on us?

Of course, we who have placed our trust in Christ for our salvation will all one day experience the physical resurrection of our bodies.

15. In order to gain some understanding of what Paul means by "[attaining] to the resurrection from the dead" in verse 11, read Colossians 2:12 and 3:1-5. According to these verses, have we already been spiritually resurrected from the dead?

If this is true, according to Romans 6:10-13, how are we to "attain to [this] resurrection" (Philippians 3:11) or to "live up to" the spiritual resurrection that "we have already attained" (Philippians 3:16)?

We have already been raised from spiritual death. It is clear that we are to live up to this truth by counting ourselves dead to sin and alive to God. In this way we spiritually "share in his sufferings" (v. 10, Romans

8:17-18) and experience the power of Christ's resurrection. And in so doing, we "live up to" the spiritual resurrection that "we have already attained" (Philippians 3:16).

16. What was it that Paul pressed on "to take hold of" (v. 12)?

Paul pressed hard after the goal of knowing Christ (v. 10) which is why Christ took hold of each one of us (that we might know Him). *We* were the joy that was set before Him when He went to the cross (Hebrews 12:2). Oh, what love! Oh, what a wonderful Savior!

17. With this in mind, what do you believe was the prize that Paul says he was pressing toward and straining to gain in verses 13-14?

The prize for Paul was Christ Himself (see verses 8-10, 20). There is no greater joy than knowing Him and being found in Him!

18. If you do not resonate with the way Paul felt about Christ, what does that tell you about your spiritual maturity (v. 15)?

19. How do we grow spiritually? Is it by becoming more disciplined? How does 2 Peter 3:18 say we are to grow?

20. If you are not at the point where you think like Paul, what can you be sure of (Philippians 3:15)?

21. We have now established that the "pattern" of Paul's life (v. 17) was to glory in Christ and what He accomplished on the cross for his daily salvation and righteousness, joy and fulfillment. In contrast, what did Paul say that those who live as enemies of the cross of Christ glory in (vv. 17-18)?

22. What do they look to for joy and fulfillment (v. 19)?

23. What are they continually thinking about (Philippians 3:19)?

We will either exalt Christ and live for Him or we will live to satisfy our own appetites (Romans 6:19-21). There is no way we can be successful at simply trying not to satisfy the desires of our sinful nature; if instead, we begin looking to Christ for fulfillment and glorying in Him, we will find that we do not gratify the desires of the sinful nature.

24. What is their destiny (Philippians 3:19)?

25. What is the destiny of those who glory in the cross of Christ (vv. 20-21)?

When we stop trusting in ourselves and our own abilities and place our confidence in the person of Christ and the same power that raised Him from the dead, we are set free to experience His resurrection power over sin and death. As a result of being liberated from our bondage, we desire nothing more than relationship with our Rescuer and being with Him for all eternity (vv. 20-21).

Week 3
Day 3: The Knowledge of God and Its Transforming Power

In Lesson 1, I stated that you cannot surrender to someone you do not *trust*. In Lesson 2, I stated that because we cannot *trust* someone we do not *know*, the knowledge of God (rather than obedience) should be our goal. In Lesson 3, I talked about how it was the revelation of God's compassion toward me in my helpless, sinful state and the knowledge of the treasure I was to Him that transformed me. From being a proud, insecure, self-focused person, I was becoming a passionate lover of Christ and others. As you read today's Scriptures, contemplate the transforming power of knowing God.

Read 2 Peter 1:1-4.

1. According to verse 2, how do we receive grace and peace?

2. Through what has His divine power given us everything we need for life and godliness (verse 3)?

3. What was Peter's last exhortation to us at the end of his books, found in 2 Peter 3:18?

Think about the fact that it is our knowledge of Him that gives us grace and peace and everything we need for life and godliness. It wasn't until I truly gained an understanding of God as a loving, kind, compassionate father that I had the ability to be truly loving, kind, and compassionate. When God removes the veil from our eyes to see who He really is, knowing who He is transforms us into His likeness.

4. How does Colossians 3:9-10 say our new self is being renewed?

5. According to 2 Corinthians 3:18, what happens to us as we look upon (or contemplate) the Lord's glory?

6. Through His glory and goodness, He has given us His very great and precious promises. According to 2 Peter 1:4, why has He done this?

Isn't it amazing that we actually participate in God's divine nature when we know and trust in His promises? By faith in His very great and precious promises, we find that all our needs are met and discover that we don't desire what this world has to offer. Reminding myself of God's character and promises actually takes care of my sin issues.

7. Which of these following statements is an accurate conclusion from 2 Peter 1:1-4? (Choose only one.)

   a. As we make obedience our focus and seek to please God in all we do, we experience grace and peace and everything we need to live life, and we become like the One in whose image we were created.
   b. As we grow in our knowledge of God, we experience grace and peace and everything we need to live life, and we become like the One in whose image we were created.

8. Which of these following statements is an accurate conclusion from 2 Peter 1:1-4? (Choose only one.)

   a. By seeking to be holy as God is holy and to keep sin out of our lives, we actually participate in His divine nature and are able to say no to the destructive desires of our flesh.
   b. By knowing and trusting in His promises, we actually participate in God's divine nature and consequently are able to say no to the destructive desires of our flesh.

Read Romans 1:18-20, 28-31.

9. What have men who suppress the truth not thought worthwhile to hold onto (v. 28)?

10. What has been the result (vv. 29-31)?

11. In light of what we have learned thus far about the knowledge of God, why is it so important to "demolish arguments and every pretension that sets itself up against the knowledge of God," as 2 Corinthians 10:5 says?

Read Romans 10:2-3.

12. What had the Jews not based their zeal for God on?

13. What was the result of their ignorance (v. 3)?

Read Jeremiah 9:23-24.

14. What did God say is the only thing worth boasting about (v. 24)?

15. How does God describe Himself in verse 24?

16. What reason does He give for exercising kindness, justice, and righteousness?

17. Read Titus 3:3-7 and describe how God has exercised these three things in what He has done for you personally (His kindness, justice, and righteousness).

God's kindness, justice, and righteousness were demonstrated toward all of us in what Christ did for us on the cross. We were "deceived and enslaved by all kinds of passions and pleasures" and therefore, God's justice required that we be punished, but His kindness, love, and mercy were expressed toward us when Christ took our punishment and justified us by His grace, washing away our sinfulness with His blood and crediting to us His righteousness. It is as we grow in our knowledge and understanding of who He is and what He has done for us that we grow in our love for Him and live out the righteousness that is ours in Christ.

Read Philippians 1:9-11.

18. How does our love abound more and more according to verse 9?

19. What is the result of knowing the depth of Christ's love (vv. 10-11)?

20. What did Paul say in Philippians 3:7-10 was his greatest passion?

Can you understand why Paul's passion was to know Christ? The more Paul knew Christ, the more he loved Him and the more passionate he became to know Him better. If you do not have a deep love in your heart for Christ, it is because you do not really know who He is and the love He has demonstrated toward you. If you have a desire to know how much Christ loves you, then seek to grow in your knowledge of who He is. Because God *is* love (1 John 4:16), in order to know His love, we have to get to know *Him*. As A. W. Tozer wrote, "To know Him is to love Him, and to know Him better is to love Him more."[14] We love Him because He first loved us; therefore, the more we know Him, the more we love Him because we realize more the depths of His love for us.

My dear sister in Christ, "I keep asking that the God of our Lord Jesus Christ, the glorious Father, may give you the Spirit of wisdom and revelation, so that you may know him better" (Ephesians 1:17). "And

I pray that you, being rooted and established in love, may have power, together with all the saints, to grasp how wide and long and high and deep is the love of Christ, and to know this love that surpasses knowledge—that you may be filled to the measure of all the fullness of God" (Ephesians 3:17-19).

21. According to Ephesians 3:19, how are we filled up with God in all His fullness?

Week 3
Day 4: John 15:1-17

Read John 15:1-17.

1. What does the Father (our gardener) do to us to make us become more fruitful (v. 2)?

The word *prunes* also means *purges* or *cleanses*.

2. How do we become clean (v. 3)?

3. In verses 4, 5, 6, 7, and 10, Jesus says, "Remain." Does remaining require work? How would you define *remain*?

To remain in Christ is simply to stay in Him. We draw our strength, wisdom, and salvation from Him when we stay connected to (or remain in) the Vine.

4. If we remain in the vine, where will He remain (v. 4)?

5. How much fruit are we able to produce apart from the Vine (vv. 4-5)?

6. How much fruit will we bear if we remain in the Vine (v. 5)?

7. What happens to us if we do not remain in the vine (v. 6)?

If we do not remain in the Vine, we become totally useless. We are completely dependent on Him to bear fruit. If we get disconnected from Him, we will wither, dry up, and become good for nothing.

8. Do you see ways in which you are disconnected from the Vine?

9. What are the areas in your life in which you feel you are disconnected from Him?

Acknowledge your helplessness in these areas and express your need for Christ by writing out a prayer to Him here.

10. What part does the Word of God play in getting our prayers answered (v. 7)?

11. Why do you suppose this is so? (see James 4:3)

12. What is the evidence that we are Jesus' disciples (v. 8)?

13. In verse 9 Jesus tells us to remain in His *love*. In our lesson this week, I stated that to remain in Christ's love means to live mindful of His love, to allow myself to be wrapped in His loving arms and receive His love. Are you trusting in Christ's great love for you, knowing that there is nothing you can do to make Him love you less and nothing you can do to make Him love you more?

14. What did Jesus say in verses 15 and 23 of John 14 that we would do if we love Him?

Jesus taught that obedience is the natural outcome of our love for Him (see also 1 John 5:3). What, then, do you think Jesus means in John 15:10 when He states, "If you obey my commands, you will remain in my love, just as I have obeyed my Father's commands and remain in his love"?

Of course, Jesus does not love us more if we obey Him. This would be contrary to all that Scripture teaches about God's grace being His unconditional favor toward undeserving man. Warren W. Wiersbe wrote, "Because we love Him, we keep His commandments; and, as we keep His commandments, we abide in His love and experience it in a deeper way."[15]

15. For what purpose did Christ say these things to His disciples (v. 11)?

16. Are you experiencing the joy of resting in Christ's love?

17. Christ gives one command in verses 12 and 17. What is this command?

18. To what degree are we to love others (v. 12)?

19. How did Christ show us the full extent of His love (v. 13; see also John 13:1)?

20. According to verses 13-15, does Christ want us to be His servants or His friends?

21. Did we choose Christ or did Christ choose us (v. 16)?

According to this verse, why did Christ choose us?

22. Remaining in Christ's great love for us transforms us. Spend some time meditating on verse 13 and the fact that Jesus laid down his life for you personally. Write this verse on a card and put it in a place where you will see it and continue to be reminded of the extent of Christ's love for you.

Week 3
Day 5: Ephesians 1-2

As you read Ephesians 1-2, underline every phrase that says "in Christ," "in Him," or "through Jesus Christ." Then write down every single thing you find in these chapters that you have by being in Christ.

Week 4
Day 2: Trusting in His Care

1. Read Jeremiah 31:3, Isaiah 46:3-4, and Isaiah 49:15. Record what these verses tell us about how God feels and acts toward His children.

Jeremiah 31:3

Isaiah 46:3-4

Isaiah 49:15

Read Hebrews 12:1-13.

2. What motivates God to discipline His children (v. 6)?

3. Whom does He punish (v. 6)?

4. When we have difficulties in our lives, what can we assume (v. 7)?

5. If you are not disciplined by God, what does that say about you (v. 8)?

6. How should we respond to the discipline of our Father (v. 9)?

7. What is His purpose in disciplining us (v. 10)?

8. If we allow our Father to teach us through the discipline, what will be the result in our lives (v. 11)?

9. The last time you went through hardship, how did you respond?

10. What did God teach you through it?

11. Did you see it as from the loving hand of your Father?

Read Isaiah 38:9, 17.

12. Why did Hezekiah say he had had to suffer anguish?

13. What did he say God had done for him during his illness?

Read Psalm 119:67-68.

14. What did David say caused him to obey God's word (v. 67)?

15. What did David believe about God even though he had been afflicted (v. 68)?

16. What did David desire for God to do (v. 68)?

17. After reading today's scriptures, what things do you need to keep in mind the next time God allows hardships in your life?

18. What truth about God, as seen in all these scriptures, can you hold onto that will "strengthen your feeble arms and weak knees" (Hebrews 12:12)?

Week 4
Day 3: Trusting in His Presence

Read each of the following scriptures and answer the questions. As you read, notice how often God calms the fears of His people with the words, "I will be with you." You may want to underline this promise each time you see it in your Bible.

Deuteronomy 31:6-8

1. What did Moses repeat to Joshua that would make him strong and courageous (vv. 6, 8)?

Joshua 1:5-9

2. What did God keep reminding Joshua that He would do for him (vv. 5, 9)?

Psalm 27:1-3

3. What gave David his confidence?

4. David calls God three things in verse 1. What are they, and what does each one mean to you?

    1.)

    2.)

    3.)

Psalm 118:6-8

5. What kept the psalmist from fear (vv. 6, 7)?

6. Where did he find refuge (v. 8)?

Isaiah 41:8-14

7. What did God keep reminding Israel?

8. Notice verse 14. The Israelites could not muster courage by trying to convince themselves that they were strong. Why do you think God addresses them as "O worm Jacob, O little Israel"?

Isaiah 43:1-7

9. What did God keep reminding Israel in these verses?

10. Why did God promise to be with the Israelites and protect them from harm (v. 4)?

Isaiah 51:12-16

11. When you begin to fear people or situations in your life, what do you need to remind yourself?

Matthew 28:19-20

12. What comforting words did Jesus say that help us to be bold in teaching others the things that God has taught us (v. 20)?

Hebrews 13:5-6

13. How can we avoid idolizing money (or anything else, for that matter)?

Week 4
Day 4: Trusting in His Love Casts Out Fear

Read Isaiah 48:17-18, 22.

1. According to these verses, why does God give us commands? (Choose only one.)

    a. because He wants to show us who is boss
    b. because He wants to make our lives difficult
    c. because He knows what is best for us and wants us to experience peace

   The answer is obviously *c*, but Satan certainly works hard to make us doubt that God's intentions are not truly good. What lies about God and His character are you tempted to believe that sometimes keep you from completely trusting Him?

2. Read Isaiah 30:1-7, 15-19. God told the people of Judah that if they would repent of their sins and rest and trust in Him, He would save them from their enemies. However, rather than trusting Him for salvation, the people of Judah turned to Egypt for help and then turned and ran from their enemies.

   Can you relate to these Israelites? Can you see any areas in your life where you are having difficulty trusting God and are consequently looking to yourself, to other people, or to something else to grant you whatever it is that you need? If so, what are these areas?

3. Read verses 18 and 19 again and write down what you learn about God's character and attitude toward you that you can cling to for deliverance from your circumstances.

4. How many are blessed who wait for Him (v. 18)?

5. How long does it take Him to answer when we cry for help (v. 19)?

Read Isaiah 54:10

6. What characteristic of God do you see in this verse that was also mentioned in Isaiah 30:18?

7. How does it make you feel to know that God has compassion on you?

8. According to Isaiah 54:10, what can one learn about the love God has for His own?

Read each of the following scriptures and answer the questions.
Psalm 16:1-2, 8

9. When a storm last hit your life, where did you turn for refuge?

10. When we are in life's storms, what will keep us from being shaken (v. 8)?

Psalm 112:6-8

11. Is there anything that you currently fear? _____ If so, what?

12. What do verses 7 and 8 say will make your heart secure and steadfast?

Isaiah 50:7-10

13. What do we need to know that will keep us steadfast (or "set our faces like flint") and keep us from fear of shame (v. 7)? The Sovereign Lord _____ _____.

14. What do we need to know that will keep us from fearing the condemning words of others or of Satan (v. 9)? The Sovereign Lord _____ _____.

15. According to verse 10, what keeps us from fearing walking in the dark?

Isaiah 26:3-9

16. What is a sign that we are trusting in God (v. 3)? We will have _____ _____. This means that when we are not at peace, what are we not doing?

17. What does verse 4 tell us about God that assures us He can be trusted?

What does it mean to you that He is "the Rock eternal"?

18. When we are having difficulty taking refuge in God, it is because we don't know Him well enough to be certain He can be trusted. Do you desire to intimately know Him? If so, can you make verse 8 and the first half of verse 9 your prayer to Him?

    After praying, ponder the words of Isaiah 30:18: "The Lord longs to be gracious to you; he rises to show you compassion" and Jesus' invitation to you in John 7:37: "If anyone is thirsty, let him come to me and drink."

19. According to Psalm 90:14, how does the Lord turn our fearful hearts into rejoicing hearts?

Week 4
Day 5: Trusting in His Salvation

Read Psalm 34.

At the time David wrote Psalm 34, he was hiding from Saul, who was trying to kill him.

1. In spite of his circumstances, David purposed to praise the Lord and encouraged others to join him in doing so (vv. 1-3). How often did he choose to praise the Lord (v. 1)?

2. Even though someone was pursuing David to take his life, what effect did his attention on the Lord have on his response to his circumstances (vv. 1-3)?

David's response to his circumstances was constant praise to the Lord!

3. What happens to the afflicted soul when he is reminded of who God is (v. 2)?

4. What did David do when he was fearful (v. 4)?

I think it is interesting that verse 4 does not say that David asked God for peace or for deliverance from his fears, but rather he looked for God Himself.

5. When David sought the Lord, what did He find to be true (verse 10)?

6. Are there any sins or circumstances that you are seeking deliverance from right now? If so, what are they?

7. Perhaps deliverance is not what you should be seeking. Read Jeremiah 29:13-14. In these verses, what does God say He will do for those Israelites who seek *Him*?

He says He will be found by them, and He also promises He will bring them back from captivity. In the same way, when we seek Him, we too will find Him and be freed from any bondage we have been experiencing (for example, bondage to fears or to sin).

8. How did God answer David (Psalm 34:4)?

9. How many fears did God deliver him from (v. 4)?

10. What two things does verse 5 say are true of the one who simply looks to the Lord?

11. Psalm 25:3 further expounds what causes a person to look to the Lord. What does this verse say keeps us from experiencing shame?
Do you feel any shame?

12. What do we never have to experience when we focus on the Lord (Psalm 34:5)?

13. What does Romans 10:11 say God will never do to the one who trusts in Christ?

What does Hebrews 12:2 say that Christ experienced when he endured the cross?

He took our shame upon Himself when He experienced death on the cross, and because He bore our shame for us, we no longer have to experience sin's shame.

14. In Psalm 34:6, David says he merely _____ and the Lord heard him and saved him from all his fears. All it took was for David to cry out. How many of his troubles did God deliver him from in response (vv. 6, 17, 19)?

15. The angel of the Lord in the Old Testament refers to Christ before He put on human flesh. Knowing this, who do the pronouns "him" and "he" refer to in verse 7?

16. So, was Matthew 28:20 the first time Christ promised to be with those who trusted in Him?

17. When we look to the Lord for satisfaction, what will we find out about Him (v. 8; 1 Peter 2:3)?

18. In verses 8 and 22, we find the secret to David's confidence and serenity. What did David do when he was fearful?

19. What did David say would be the benefit of placing our complete trust in God, making Him our place of refuge (v. 8)?

20. According to Scofield, "'the fear of the Lord' is an Old Testament expression meaning *reverential trust*, including the hatred of evil."[16] If we fear the Lord, what will we have to do without (v. 9)?

21. Do you have the feeling that if you surrender to the Lord you will miss out on something?

In Matthew 7:7-8 Jesus said that everyone who seeks _____. What does Psalm 34:10 and Psalm 84:11-12 say is true in reality for those who seek the Lord and surrender to Him in trust?

22. What does this tell you about God?

23. Verses 11-14 teach us what it looks like to fear the Lord. Describe the conduct of a person who fears the Lord (vv. 13-14).

24. What are the results of this conduct (vv. 12, 15)?

25. What will be the outcome of those whose conduct is wicked (v. 16)?

26. In verse 15, David says the eyes of the Lord are on the righteous and that He listens for their cry. What makes us righteous according to Romans 3:22 and 4:5?
    Does God see you as righteous? Yes / No
    Who is the only one we can credit for our righteousness (Philippians 3:9; Psalm 34:2)?

27. How many of your troubles will the Lord deliver you from (Psalm 34:17, 19)?

28. Read verse 18, Psalm 51:17, Psalm 145:18, Isaiah 57:15, Matthew 5:3-4, and James 4:6. All these verses teach us something about God and something about those whom His heart is drawn near to. What do these verses teach about God?

What do they teach about those who receive His help?

29. Would you say these words are descriptive of you: "broken hearted," "crushed in spirit," "broken by your sin," "contrite," and "humble"? If so, do you find yourself crying out to God for help?

30. According to Isaiah 57:15, why does the Lord draw close to the brokenhearted (or "contrite and lowly in spirit")?

31. What should understanding our complete helplessness cause us to do (Psalm 34:8, 22)?

32. Do verses 19-20 teach that a righteous person will not have difficulties? Yes / No

33. What does the first part of verse 19 actually say is true of a righteous person?

34. Though this is true, what are the righteous guaranteed (vv. 17, 19)?

35. Who will be condemned (v. 21)?

36. Who will not be condemned, but redeemed (v. 22)?

37. There is no shame (v. 5), no condemnation (v. 22) for those who take refuge in God. Read 1 Peter 2:6, Romans 8:1, and Hebrews 12:2, and explain why this is so.

38. Read Romans 8:33-34, rejoicing in what God has done for you as David did in Psalm 34. Look to Him for your salvation today, and let His praise be on your lips all day long.

Week 5
Days 2-4

Lies I Believe   **Truth That Can Set Me Free**

Lies I Believe

Truth That Can Set Me Free

Week 5
Day 5: Psalm 119
The Word of God, My Daily Food

After reading each of the following groups of verses from Psalm 119, write down the common theme that the psalmist communicates in each group:

1. Psalm 119:9, 11, 133 _____
2. Psalm 119:32, 45 _____
3. Psalm 119:25, 37, 40, 50, 93, 107, 149, 154, 156 _____
_____
4. Psalm 119:89, 91, 152, 160 _____
5. Psalm 119:50, 52, 82 _____
6. Psalm 119:98, 99, 100, 104, 130, 169 _____
_____
7. Psalm 119:28, 116, 175 _____
_____
8. Psalm 119:15, 23, 27, 48, 78, 95, 97, 99, 148 _____
_____
9. Psalm 119:42, 86, 138 _____
10. Psalm 119:43, 49, 74, 81, 114, 147 _____
_____
11. Psalm 119:14, 16, 24, 35, 47, 70, 77, 92, 103, 111, 143, 162, 174 _____
_____
12. Psalm 119:20, 72, 97, 113, 119, 127, 140, 159, 163, 167 _____
_____

Now look over the list of truths about what God's word accomplishes for us. Are you allowing the Word of God to perform these things in your life? Circle each truth that you currently feel a particular need for the Word of God to do in your life. Put an asterisk next to each practice of or attitude toward the Word of God that you need to develop.

In case you want to check your work from the previous page, here are the themes the psalmist communicates in each group of verses you read:

1. Your word keeps me from sin.
2. Your word brings me freedom.
3. Your word preserves my life.
4. Your word is eternal; it will endure forever.
5. Your word comforts me.

6. Your word gives me wisdom and understanding.

7. Your word strengthens and sustains me.

8. I meditate on your word.

9. I trust in your word; it is trustworthy.

10. I have put my hope in your word.

11. I delight in your word.

12. I love your word.

If you have not yet found the Word of God to be all this for you, will you ask God to give you a hunger and thirst for it? Sometimes we first have to discipline ourselves to consume something before acquiring a taste for it. Perhaps this is what you will need to do for a while with the Word of God, but I can assure you that if you persevere in spending time in God's Word, it will reveal the lies you believe, renew your mind by transforming the way you think, and become life and breath for you.

> "For the word of God is living and active. Sharper than any double-edged sword, it penetrates even to dividing soul and spirit, joints and marrow; it judges the thoughts and attitudes of the heart." (Hebrews 4:12)

> "When your words came, I ate them; they were my joy and my heart's delight, for I bear your name, O Lord God Almighty." (Jeremiah 15:16)

Week 6
Day 2: Psalm 86:11; Hebrews 3:7-4:16; Psalm 103:7-18;
Exodus 33:12-34:7; Psalm 25:4-10

1. List eight characteristics of God that you feel best describe the ways in which He deals with you.

    1.)

    2.)

    3.)

    4.)

    5.)

    6.)

    7.)

    8.)

As you read today's scriptures, notice the relationship between understanding God's ways and entering His rest.

Read Psalm 86:11.

2. What does David say he will be able to do if he is taught God's way?

Read Hebrews 3:7-4:16.[§]

[§] Hebrews 3:7-11 is a quotation taken from Psalm 95:7-11

3. According to Hebrews 3:10-11, for what two reasons could the Israelites not enter God's rest?

   1.)
   2.)

4. In Hebrews 3:19, what reason is given for the Israelites not entering God's rest?

5. How do we enter His rest according to Hebrews 4:3?

6. What does Hebrews 4:10 say happens when we enter God's rest?

This verse says that we rest from our own work when we enter God's rest. The "rest" talked about here is what we experience when we simply trust in the finished work of Christ to do for us what we could never do for ourselves. Remember what you read yesterday in Hebrews 10:12-14; according to those verses, the work of salvation for us was completely accomplished by Christ's death and resurrection. Simply trusting in Him and His character causes us to stop striving to save ourselves from sinning. Human effort can never make us righteous in God's sight. Rather, knowing and trusting in His character and what it has driven Him to accomplish for us is what transforms us into His likeness.

7. According to Hebrews 4:11, what are we to make every effort to do?

8. What does Hebrews 4:14 say that we are to hold firmly to?

9. According to Hebrews 3:10-11, knowing God's ways is key to entering into His rest. Read Psalm 103:7. What does this verse say that God made known to Moses?

10. Read the description of God's ways found in Psalm 103:8-18. List them below.

Read Exodus 33:12-34:7.

11. In Exodus 33:13, what did Moses ask God to teach him? _____ _____ (This is the same Hebrew word used in Psalm 86:11; 103:7; 95:10.)

12. Why did Moses want to know God's ways (v. 13)?

13. In verse 14, what was God's response to Moses?

There is a correlation between understanding God's ways and finding rest.

14. List how God describes His ways in Exodus 34:6-7.

15. Compare this list to the description of His ways in Psalm 103:8-18. (Refer to your answer to #10.) Underline or highlight the similarities you see between the two lists.

Read Psalm 25:4-10.

16. In Psalm 25:4, what does David ask God to show him?

17. Because the Lord is good and upright, what does He instruct sinners in, according to verse 8?

18. What does He teach the humble (v. 9)?

19. According to verse 10, what are God's ways like for those who keep His commands?

20. In Jeremiah 9:24, what does God say a person can truly have reason to boast about?

21. How does God describe Himself in this verse?

   The way you view God is directly related to your ability to trust Him. For years, I viewed God as my judge and did not understand that because of the finished work of Christ, God no longer views me as a sinner but as a beloved child.

Look back at your description of God's character that you wrote down in question #1 (pg. 157). Are the descriptions of God's ways listed in Psalm 103:8-18, Exodus 34:6-7, Psalm 25:10, and Jeremiah 9:24 consistent with the way you view God? Yes / No

If not, meditate on His ways and allow Him to alter your view of Him. When we know His ways (Hebrews 3:10) and trust in who He says He is, we enter into spiritual rest. Believing that God is compassionate, gracious, slow to anger, abounding in love, merciful, forgiving, patient, and understanding of our weakness actually transforms us from trying to perform for Him into resting in who He is, what He has done for us, and what He can do through us. And when we stray from Him, our hearts are drawn back to Him when we are reminded of His loving character. First John 4:19 says that we love Him because He first loved us. If you do not feel love in your heart for God, you need only become familiar with (or remind yourself of) His loving ways, and the knowledge of His great love for you will fill your heart with love for Him in return.

Week 6
Day 3: Romans 3

Read Romans 3.

1. According to verses 3-5, how does God respond when we lack faith and fall into sin? (Put a check by the correct answer.)

    _____ God gets angry and turns His back on us.
    _____ God is too busy to notice.
    _____ God remains faithful to us.

2. Verse 4 contains a quotation from Psalm 51, which is a psalm that David wrote after committing adultery with Bathsheba. Read Psalm 51:4, and then read Romans 3:3-5 again. Describe in your own words what is meant by: "So that you may be proved right when you speak and prevail when you judge."

Psalm 51:4 in the *Common English Bible* says, "I've sinned against you—you alone. I've committed evil in your sight. That's why you are justified when you render your verdict, completely correct when you issue your judgment."

Our sin does not change the character of God. He remains faithful when we are faithless (2 Timothy 2:13). The holiness and righteousness of God, when contrasted by our sin, are seen more clearly, and the result is that we see how far short of His glory we fall.

3. Read verses 5-20.

    1.) How many people are righteous (v. 10)? _____
    2.) Is anyone able to do good (v. 12)? _____
    3.) Can anyone become righteous in God's sight by keeping the law (v. 20)? _____

If you answered "none" to the first question and "no" to the second and third, you answered correctly. Stop and think about this reality. Do you truly believe that there is nothing good in you? Do you really understand that there is nothing you can do to please God or make yourself acceptable to Him in any way? Understanding our helplessness is key to appreciating Christ and what He has done for us to make us righteous, acceptable, and pleasing to God.

4. Read verses 10-18 again, this time keeping in mind that you and I are the ones being described. Do you really believe that apart from Christ, God sees absolutely no good in you? (See also Romans 7:18.)

5. What was the purpose of the law (vv. 19-20)?

Read verses 21-31.

6. How are we made righteous according to verses 22, 24-28, and 30?

7. Where does our righteousness come from (vv. 21-22)?

8. Who is our righteousness? (See 1 Corinthians 1:30.)

9. If we are made righteous by faith in Christ's sacrifice of Himself for us on the cross, do we have any reason to be proud of our righteousness (v. 27)?

10. As you lived your life this past week, what would you say was your primary focus?

   _____ Getting victory over sin
   _____ Living for myself
   _____ Christ as my only source of hope, righteousness, and peace

   Focusing on overcoming sin is as great a pitfall as living for ourselves because we can never overcome sin. We are incapable of it! However, as we look to Christ as our source of fulfillment, He meets the needs of our hearts and produces His righteousness in us.

11. Read Psalm 116:1-7 as a prayer of gratitude to your Savior.

Week 6
Day 4: Romans 4

1. Read Romans 4. As you read, underline all forms of the words "believe," "trust," and "faith."

    Forms of the word *justify* are used twice in this chapter. According to *Strong's Exhaustive Concordance*,[17] *justify* means "to render (show or regard as) just or innocent." Put simply, the word *justify* means "to declare righteous."

2. What two Old Testament characters mentioned in this chapter were declared righteous because of their faith?

3. According to verse 5, how is a person justified?

    This is important to understand. As believers in Christ, we can begin to look at the things we do or do not do as indications of our spirituality or righteousness, but verse 5 teaches that trusting God is the thing that God credits to us as righteousness.

    You may want to read Psalm 32 for the context of the passage that is quoted in Romans 4:7-8.

4. In Psalm 32:10, David points out what causes the Lord to cover our sins and never count them against us. What was necessary for David to do to experience God's unfailing love and forgiveness? (Hint: the Lord's unfailing love surrounds the person who does this.)

5. According to Romans 4:11-12, how is righteousness credited to us?

6. According to verse 13, how are we made righteous?

7. If God's requirement for us to gain righteousness were to keep a set standard of rules, what does verse 15 say we would bring upon ourselves?

8. What is the promise that is talked about in verse 16? (Refer back to verse 13.)

9. How did Abraham receive that promise, according to verse 13?

10. How do we receive it, according to verse 16?

11. Verse 17 says that God "gives life to the dead and calls things that are not as though they were." What did Romans 3:10 make clear that we are not?

12. According to Romans 4:5-6 and Romans 3:28, what does God declare that we are if we have placed our faith in Him?

13. Read Romans 4:24-25 again and explain how a holy God can credit us as sinners with righteousness (4:24-25).

14. Spend some time rejoicing and thanking God for the way He now views you and for what Christ has done for you to make you righteous.

Week 6
Day 5: Galatians 3

Read Galatians 3. As you read, underline all forms of the words *believe* and *faith*.

1. Paul asks this question of the Galatians in verse 1: "Who has bewitched you?" What does the word *bewitched* indicate to you?

2. Paul was writing to people who had believed in Christ for their salvation. Are you beginning to see any ways in which Satan has diverted your attention from God's grace to trusting in your own ability? If so, write out the ways in which you now see he has done this.

3. How did you receive the Spirit of God (v. 2)?

4. If we received the Spirit by faith, then how are we to continue to live (refer to verses 2-3 and Colossians 2:6)?

5. For a long time I tried in vain to overcome sin in my life. I was consumed with trying to be good and holy because I thought that was what I needed to do to please God as a Christian. Galatians 3:5-12 tells us how we are actually made righteous. What is repeated over and over that makes us righteous in God's sight? (Hint: I asked you to underline the words in your Bible.)

6. Verses 6-18 make it clear that Abraham's belief in God was credited to him as righteousness and that he received the promised inheritance simply because of faith in God's promise, not because of anything he had done or obedience to the law. Put simply, God's promises to Abraham were unconditional, not based on anything Abraham had to do. The righteousness that Christ has given us is also unconditional. We cannot do anything to attain it. If we could, then we could say as Christians that we have something to boast about, that we have brought about our own spiritual maturity, or that we have done something to gain God's approval. This is the lie that Satan attempts to make Christians believe. Read the following verses and write what God has to say about His unconditional grace and favor toward us:

    2 Timothy 2:13

    1 Corinthians 15:10

For years I believed that I had a positional standing of righteousness before God but thought that I had to live righteously in order to gain God's pleasure and favor toward me as a Christian. I failed to see that faith in this positional standing of righteousness actually produces righteous living. As I understand that I already have God's pleasure and favor and do not have to do anything to gain it, the joy and rest that His complete acceptance brings to my soul actually keeps me from being drawn to the sins that once seemed so attractive. Notice Paul said in 1 Corinthians 15:10 that he was what he was *by the grace of God*. It was actually the grace of God that produced the righteousness in him.

7. Galatians 3:23 describes us as being held prisoners by the law before faith was revealed. Do you feel imprisoned by any set of rules? Have you actually become a slave to obedience (as I had) rather than to Christ Himself?

8. Verse 24 says that the purpose of the law was to lead us to Christ. If I had not understood that God actually demands perfection, I would never have understood that I could not attain to His standard. If you are attempting to live up to what you believe God expects of you as a Christian, you will end up doing one of two things: either you will run to Christ for help knowing you cannot do it yourself, or you will lower God's standard so that you do not feel bad about yourself. Do you see yourself doing one of these two things? Which one?

9. Can you see how understanding the grace of God actually upholds the law (Romans 3:31)? Romans 7:12 says that "the law is holy, and the commandment is holy, righteous, and good." In His grace, God says to us, *You don't have to do this. I will do it for you!* However, if we attempt to attain God's standard of righteousness ourselves, we actually lower His standard because we cannot attain perfection. It is important to understand that the grace of God does not make it possible for us to live at a lower standard of righteousness. Rather, it gives us the opportunity to run to Christ, the only one who can keep God's standard of righteousness. This is why verse 25 says, "Now that faith has come, we are no longer under the supervision of the law." What do you think this means?

Neither the law nor any set of rules governs us. Christ has set us free!

10. How do we become sons of God, according to verse 26?

11. With whom are we now clothed (v. 27)?

12. Being clothed with Christ means we are clothed with His righteousness. (See number 16 on pages 124-125.) Describe how trusting that this is true will make a difference in your life.

13. Have you been striving to do all that you think God expects of you as a Christian? Yes / No Read Galatians 2:20-21 as a statement of your faith in Christ and rest in the righteousness that you have already been given.

Week 7
Day 2: Hebrews 9

Hebrews 9 has been one of the most liberating chapters in the Bible for me. It played a crucial role in understanding the finished work of Christ and what it had accomplished for me. It was one of the primary passages God used to set me free from the bondage of trying to make myself pleasing to Him as a Christian. This passage points us to Christ as our only hope and salvation in being pleasing to God. Read Hebrews 9.

1. Who alone was allowed to enter the inner room of the sanctuary, called the Most Holy Place (v. 7)?

2. What was the high priest always required to offer, both for himself and for the sins of the people, when he entered the Most Holy Place (v. 7)?

3. How often did he have to do this (v. 7)?

4. Why did the Spirit of God require that only the high priest do this (v. 8)?

5. Why did the high priest have to offer blood every year (vv. 9-10)?

6. Who did the earthly high priest actually represent (v. 11)?

7. What did the Most Holy Place in the physical tabernacle represent (vv. 11-12, 24)?

8. By what means did Christ enter the Most Holy Place as our High Priest (v. 12)?

9. What type of redemption does verse 12 say that Christ obtained for us?

10. How many times did Christ have to enter the Most Holy Place (vv. 12, 25-28)?

11. Notice the tense of the verbs *entered* and *obtained* in verse 12. What does the tense of the verbs indicate to you?

12. What do the terms *eternal* and *once for all* indicate to you (vv. 12, 26)?

13. What did the priests have to sprinkle on themselves before entering the Most Holy Place (v. 13)?

14. What did the law require that Moses sprinkle on the book of the law, the people, the tabernacle, and everything used in its ceremonies (vv. 18-22)?

15. What did Christ offer when he entered the Most Holy Place (the presence of God the Father) (v. 12)?

16. Read Matthew 26:28 and Hebrews 9:22. Why did Christ offer His own blood?

17. Read Exodus 26:33, Matthew 27:50-51, and Hebrews 10:19-20. What happened on earth at the moment of Christ's death to signify to us what was taking place?

18. What did He say as He breathed His last breath (John 19:30)? ____ ____ _____

Don't miss the implications of what took place when Christ offered Himself. The past tense of the verbs in Hebrews 9:12 indicate that *the work of saving mankind was finished*. Completely accomplished, once and for all. This means that there is nothing left for us to do to make ourselves acceptable to God. We can stand with confidence in the presence of a holy God (Hebrews 4:16) because Christ sealed our eternal salvation with His death on the cross and entered one time into the presence of the Father to offer His own blood *for the forgiveness of our sins*. If Christ offered His own blood for our sins, there is nothing left for us to do to be forgiven. We are totally cleansed and pure in God's sight because the blood of Christ has cleansed us from all our sins—past, present, and future sins. The veil separating us from the Father has been torn, and we have full access to Him. Hallelujah!

Week 7
Day 3: Hebrews 10:1-25

Read Hebrews 10:1-25.

1. Verse 1 says, "The law is only a shadow of the good things that are coming—not the realities themselves." Who does Colossians 2:16-17 say that the law was pointing us to?

2. The law required that sacrifices for sins be made repeatedly. Why was this necessary (vv. 1-4)?

3. Was God pleased with these sacrifices (v. 6)?

4. Are there things you are doing in an effort to please God or to receive His forgiveness?
    If so, what are they?

    Even though the law required that sacrifices and offerings be made (v. 8), God was not pleased with them.

5. Who came to do God's will (vv. 5-7, 9)? _____

6. Read Luke 22:42 and John 18:11. What was the Father's will (Hebrews 10:10)?

7. According to *Strong's Exhaustive Concordance*,[18] the Greek word for *will* in Hebrews 10:7, 9, 10 is defined as "a determination, choice, or inclination," and this word can be translated as *desire, pleasure,* or *will*. This same Greek word is used in Ephesians 1:5. Read Ephesians 1:3-6. What does Ephesians 1:5 tell us was the Father's will?

8. What motivated the Father to desire this for us (Ephesians 1:4, 1 John 3:1)?

9. Hebrews 10:11-14 compares the repeated sacrifices the earthly priests had to offer with the one sacrifice Christ offered. Why do you suppose the Holy Spirit compelled the author of Hebrews to keep emphasizing that it was only necessary for Christ to be sacrificed once?

10. Satan works hard at trying to get us to think we can do what only Christ can do, that Christ's sacrifice was not enough. As a believer in Christ for my salvation from eternal hell, I believed in a subtle way that it was up to me to make myself righteous as a Christian. I did not even realize that this was what I was doing; however, when I was intent on obeying God in order to make myself

acceptable to Him, I was not trusting that Christ had already made me acceptable. I also thought I had to ask God to forgive my sins that I was committing on a daily basis in order to be forgiven when in reality, I was already forgiven. These are ways in which Satan had me deceived into believing that it was really up to me to gain acceptance with God. What "sacrifices" are you still trying to offer to God to make yourself acceptable to Him?

11. Verses 16-17 are quotes taken from Jeremiah 31:33-34. Read Jeremiah 31:31-34. Why did God have to make a new covenant with Israel (Jeremiah 31:32)?

12. What was the new covenant He made with Israel (Jeremiah 31:33-34)?

13. According to Romans 11:26-27, with whom besides the physical descendants of Israel has God made this covenant?

14. What did God say was His relationship to Israel (Jeremiah 31:32)?

15. To whom is Christ a husband according to Ephesians 5:22-32?

16. Read Matthew 26:27-28. What did Jesus call the cup He offered to His disciples to drink from?

17. Why did He say His blood would be poured out (Matthew 26:28)?

18. Because Christ's blood was poured out for the forgiveness of our sins, what does Hebrews 10:18 say still needs to be done in order for us to be forgiven?

19. According to Hebrews 10:19, what does the shed blood of Christ make possible for us to do?

20. In verses 19-25 the writer of Hebrews says that the confidence that we have through Christ's blood to enter the presence of the Father and the fact that we have a high priest who Himself speaks to the Father on our behalf give us the ability to do five things. What are these five things? (They are listed in verses 22-25. Each one begins with "let us.")

   1.)
   2.)
   3.)
   4.)
   5.)

Do you see how everything we are called to do and be as Christians can only be done as we look to Christ and the work that He has accomplished for us? Fix your eyes on Him and rest in His finished work on your behalf today.

Week 7
Day 4: Romans 2

Read Romans 2.

1. Why is it that when we judge others we are really condemning ourselves (v. 1)?

Do you really believe that this is true, or do you find yourself judging others with the feeling that you are better than they are?

2. What does Romans 3:9 say is true about the whole world?

3. Who only has the ability to rightly judge others (Romans 2:2)?
   Why is this true?

4. Read Matthew 7:1-5. What do these verses and Romans 2:3, 5-6 tell us will happen to the one who passes judgment on others?

5. Examining myself before looking at others helps me be full of mercy for others because I can easily see that I, too, am deserving of judgment apart from Christ. If I do not recognize my own sinfulness, what am I turning a blind eye to and actually showing contempt for (Romans 2:4)?

6. According to verse 4, what brings us to repentance?

7. What do verses 6-10 say that God will judge all of us for?

8. According to Romans 3:10, 12, have any of us done good?

9. If God is going to judge all of us for what we have done, what would be the verdict for all of us apart from Christ (verses 8-9)?

10. Read James 2:8-26. What does this passage teach about the connection between faith and deeds?

11. We already learned from Romans 3:9-12 and 19 that none of us is capable of doing what is good. Yet, James teaches us that there is a way to truly do good deeds in God's sight. How is that? (Refer also to Hebrews 11:5-6.)

12. As a reminder, write what John 15:5 says we can do apart from Christ.

And how do we bear fruit, according to John 15:4?

13. If Christ is the only One who can produce anything good in us, then when we are judging others, what have we forgotten?

14. In Romans 3:20, Paul explains that no one will be declared righteous in God's sight by observing the law. Why, then, in Romans 2:13 does he say that it is those who obey the law who will be declared righteous?

    Paul is saying that if we *could* keep the law, we would, in fact, be righteous in God's sight.

15. Because the Jews prided themselves in being entrusted with the law of God, Paul explains to them in Romans 2:9-28 that hearing the law is very different from keeping the law. What does he point out to the Jews in verses 17-27?

    Paul is showing the Jews in these verses that they have not kept the law; and because they have put themselves under the law, they will be judged by the law (v. 12).

16. We as Christians are not so unlike the Jews. We can begin to think that because we do not do certain things, we are better than others. In reality, however, we either do the same things in our hearts as those we judge or we disobey God in other areas, making us equally guilty before God. We also can think that just because we are familiar with truth that we have submitted ourselves to it. Are you guilty of thinking any of these thoughts? If so, what specifically are you guilty of thinking?

17. The Jews also believed that circumcision put them in right standing with God. What does Paul say would cause circumcision to be of no significance for them whatsoever (v. 25)?

18. According to Romans 4:11, what was circumcision a sign of?

19. Read Galatians 6:12-15. What was the reason certain Jews were pressuring others to be circumcised (vv. 12-13)?

20. What did Paul say was the only thing he wanted to boast about (Galatians 6:14)?

21. Can you relate to Paul's passion? What do you most find joy in and want to boast about?

22. Paul said that circumcision was not anything of significance. What did he say was the only thing that mattered (Galatians 6:15)?

23. Read Colossians 2:11-13. According to verse 11, what is meant by the circumcision of the heart that is talked about in Romans 2:28-29? (For help, look ahead to #26.)

24. Read Deuteronomy 30:6. Who circumcises our hearts (see also Colossians 2:11)?

25. What important word do you see in Colossians 2:12 that is also in Romans 4:11?

    We are spiritually circumcised by faith, just as Abraham received the sign of circumcision as a seal of the righteousness he had by faith.

26. Because of our faith in Christ, He has set us free (or "circumcised" us) from the sinful nature. According to Deuteronomy 30:6, what is the result of our being set free?

Week 7
Day 5: Galatians 3:26-5:16

Read Galatians 3:26-5:16.

1. In what way is a child no different from a slave (4:1-3)?

2. When we were children (spiritually speaking), what were we in slavery to (v. 3)?

3. What does Galatians 4:9-10 and Colossians 2:8, 20-23 say are some of the principles (or rules) that this world gives us?

What does Colossians 2:22 say these principles are based upon?

Human logic can cause us to think that the way to overcome sin is by becoming disciplined and submitting to rules, but of what value does Paul say that these regulations truly are in restraining our sinful nature (Colossians 2:23)?

4. What was true of us when we were children and under rules and regulations (Galatians 4:3)? We were in _____.

5. What happened that enabled us to receive our full rights as sons (vv. 4-5)?

6. Whose Spirit did God send into our hearts because we are His sons (v. 6)? He sent the Spirit of _____ _____ into our hearts. It is natural for the Spirit of Christ to call God "Father." Read Romans 8:15. By whom do we also call Him "Father"?

7. Why are we able to call Him "Father" (Galatians 4:5)? Like Christ does, we have the full rights _____ _____.

8. Galatians 4:7 says that as sons we have also been made _____. Read Romans 8:17. According to this verse, what are we heirs of?

As an heir, everything that is God's is mine, and God Himself is mine!

9. What had the Galatians begun doing (Galatians 4:9-10) that Paul said would put them in slavery again?

Examine your own heart. Are there rules and regulations in your life that you have become enslaved to? Yes / No

If so, what are they?

10. What happened to the Galatians as a result of turning back to observing rules and regulations (v. 15)?

Are you experiencing joy in Christ for all that He has done for you? Yes / No

If not, why not? Could it be because you have turned to "weak and miserable principles" in trying to make yourself pleasing to God?

11. What was Paul in anguish over in verse 19?

12. Paul was talking to people who had become sons of God (verses 6-7). What do you think He meant by the words "until Christ is formed in you" in verse 19?

According to 1 Corinthians 1:30, who is our righteousness, holiness, and redemption?

What are you looking to for your righteousness, holiness, and redemption? Are you looking to any rules or regulations rather than to Christ?

Christ is "formed" in us when we are trusting in Him alone for our righteousness and salvation. He will not share His glory with any other idol—not even the idol of obedience.

13. In Galatians 4:21-5:1, Paul tells us that Ishmael (who was born "in the ordinary way" by a slave woman named Hagar whom Sarah gave to Abraham as a concubine in order that he might have a child) can figuratively represent the Jews who are in slavery to the law, and that Isaac (whom Sarah gave birth to as a result of God's promise) can figuratively represent those who have been born into God's family on the basis of what Christ has done for them.

    Read Galatians 5:11. What did Ishmael do to Isaac that those who are under rules and regulations do to those who are living in freedom in Christ (Galatians 4:29)?

This persecution is a clear indication that legalism and trusting in Christ stand in opposition to one another. We are either trusting in Christ's righteousness or in our own. There is no middle ground.

14. What does Galatians 4:30 teach us that only those who are born by the power of the Spirit will receive? (See also Romans 4:13-14.)

15. What does Galatians 5:1 tell us was the reason Christ set us free?

16. In verses 2-3, Paul says that Christ will be of no value at all to those who trust in circumcision to be in right standing with God. Is there anything that you as a Christian are trusting in (besides Christ) to make yourself acceptable to God? Yes / No
    If so, what does this tell you is true about Christ who lives in you?

17. In verse 4, who does Paul say we have been alienated from if we are trying to be righteous by observing the law?
    What is the other way he describes trying to be justified by law (v. 4)? He says that those who do so have _____ _____ _____ _____. Falling away from grace means that we are trusting in something other than the grace of God to make us righteous.

18. How do we gain righteousness (v. 5)?

19. What does verse 6 say is the only thing that counts?

20. If we are being persuaded to conform to any set of rules or to work harder as Christians to be more like Christ, who is this persuasion *not* coming from (verses 7-8)?

21. In light of the context (verses 1-8), what do you think is meant by "A little yeast works through the whole batch of dough" (v. 9)?

What do we need to throw out in order to keep our faith in Christ pure (see 4:30)?

Paul is saying that we cannot allow conformity to the law or to any set of rules creep into our lives.

22. Why is the cross offensive to legalists (v. 11)?

The cross was offensive to those who preached circumcision or adherence to any set of rules for salvation because the cross meant they could no longer take pride in attaining their own salvation.

23. What were we called to be (v. 13)?

Does this mean we can live like we want to (v. 13)? Yes / No
What are we commanded to do instead (vv. 13-14)?

24. Paul has just talked for five-and-a-half chapters about the error in trying to be justified by keeping the law, so we can be sure that he is not telling us that we are to love others in order to gain a right standing with God. To the contrary, who gives us the ability to love others (Galatians 5:16, 22)?
 How are we able to love others according to 1 John 4:19?

We can conclude that it is Christ who puts us in right standing with God and it is also Christ who produces the fruit of righteousness in our daily lives. The only thing required of us is to believe this. Take a moment to thank Christ for His mighty power to save.

Week 8
Day 2: Ephesians 3; 1 John 4:11-19

Read Ephesians 3.

1. How did Paul say he had become a servant of the gospel (v. 7)? He said, "I became a servant of this gospel by the _____ ___ _____ _____ _____ ___ . . ."

2. Whose power was at work to give him this grace (v. 7)?

3. What specifically was the grace given him (vv. 8-9)?

Remember that God's grace is His giving to us what we do not deserve. Why did Paul feel he did not deserve to preach the unsearchable riches of Christ (v. 8)?
    Compare verse 8 to 1 Corinthians 15:9-10. Paul's writings exude gratitude to Christ and love for Him. What did Paul's realization of what he had done and his own sinfulness have to do with this?

Do you have a deep gratitude to Christ and love for Him in your heart?
    If not, could it be because you do not realize how sinful and undeserving you are?

4. Ephesians 3:11 says that God has accomplished His eternal purpose. In whom does it say that He accomplished it? He accomplished it in _____ _____ _____ _____.

5. According to verse 12 and Ephesians 1:4-5, what was His eternal purpose?

This is an amazing reality! Knowing for all eternity that men would become slaves to sin and separated from Him by that sin, God had a plan to make us His holy and blameless children and to provide a way for us to enter His presence freely and boldly.

6. What is the reason we are able to approach God with freedom and confidence (v. 11-12)?

7. In verses 14-19, Paul prays for the Ephesians. As you fill in the following blanks, notice what he asks God the Father for:

    "I pray that out of his glorious riches he may _____ you with _____ through _____ _____ in your inner being, so that _____ may _____ in your hearts through _____. And I pray that you, being rooted and established in _____, may have _____, together with all the saints, to grasp how _____ and _____ and _____ and _____ is the _____ of _____, and to _____ this _____ that surpasses knowledge—that you may be _____ to the measure of all the _____ of _____."

8. How does the Father strengthen us with power in our inner being (v. 16)? He does so through _____ _____.

Ephesians 3:17 talks about Christ dwelling in our hearts; compare this to John 15:4, where Jesus said, "Abide in me, and I in you" (KJV). It is interesting that both Paul, in writing to Christians, and Jesus, in talking to His disciples who had believed in Him, talk about Christ dwelling (or abiding) in their hearts. Though we know that the Spirit of Christ lives in every person who belongs to Christ (Romans 8:9), Christ told His disciples that if they would abide in Him, He would abide in them also. Likewise, Paul prayed for the Ephesian Christians that Christ might dwell in them.

9. How does Christ dwell in the hearts of believers, according to verse 17? Christ dwells in our hearts through _____.

We can conclude then that abiding (remaining) in Christ happens as we live in complete trust and dependence on Him.

10. Compare Ephesians 3:17-19 with John 15:9-13. Do you see any similarities between these verses? If so, what?

What did Paul pray that the Ephesians would be rooted and established in (Ephesians 3:17)?
What did Jesus tell His disciples to remain in (John 15:9)?
Ephesians 3:17-19 describes how we may be "filled to the measure of all the fullness of God" (in other words, how we may be filled with the Spirit of God). How is that, according to these verses?

These verses teach that we are filled with all the fullness of God when we are rooted and established in Christ's love, grasping how beyond measure and beyond comprehension is that love. Since this is true, then when we are not filled with the Spirit but are tempted to live according to our sinful desires, what can we conclude will keep us from fulfilling those sinful desires?

Reminding ourselves of God's *love* for us will keep us from falling into sin. When we trust in His great love for us, we find ourselves satisfied with His love, and sin loses its appeal. God Himself fills up all the empty places of unmet needs in our lives, and we long for nothing more.

11. Read 1 John 4:11-19. What words do you see in vv. 12-13 that are similar to what Paul prayed in Ephesians 3:17 and what Jesus said in John 15:4?

    If you answered *love* and *live*, you answered correctly. The exact Greek word that is used in 1 John 4:12, 13, 15, 16 (translated "live" and "lives" in the NIV) is used in John 15:4 (translated "remain" in the NIV). A similar word is used in Ephesians 3:17 (translated "dwell" in the NIV).

12. Do you see any further similarities in 1 John 4:11-19, Ephesians 3:16-19, and John 15:9-13? If so, what?

Like Ephesians 3 and John 15, 1 John 4:11-19 talks about knowing and relying on the love that God has for us. We can see from all of these passages that as we trust in His great love, we live in Him and He lives in us.

Do you see how "knowing and relying on the love of God" (1 John 4:16) causes us to "be filled to the measure of all the fullness of God" (Ephesians 3:19)?

13. Spend some time meditating on the great love that God has for you by reading Romans 8:31-39. Visualize yourself being held and shielded by the magnificent arms of God.

    As you rest in complete trust in Him today, you will see Him "do immeasurably more than all [you] ask or imagine, according to his power that is at work within [you]" (Ephesians 3:20)!

Week 8
Day 3: Romans 5

Read Romans 5, underlining the words "faith," "gift," and "grace" as you read.

1. Look back (Week 6, Day 4, p. 163) at the definition of *justify* from *Strong's Exhaustive Concordance*. Write in your own words what the word *justified* in verses 1 and 9 of Romans 5 means.

2. Verses 1 and 2 say there are two things we now have as a result of being declared righteous. What are they?

    1. _____ with God (or literally, "facing God") through our Lord Jesus Christ
    2. Access into _____

    As we talked about in Lesson 7, grace can be defined as receiving what we do not deserve.

3. What does verse 2 say we now stand in? _____
    What does it mean to "stand in grace" (refer to Lesson 8, p. 89)?

4. What has God poured out into our hearts (v. 5)?

5. What do verses 6-8 say God demonstrated for us when we were powerless to do anything to be reconciled to Him?

6. How did God display His great love for us (v. 6)?

Verses 6-8 describe how, when we were powerless to do anything to be reconciled to God, He displayed His great love for us by sending His Son to die for us so that we might have a relationship with God.

7. Verses 9-11 compare what He did for us before we were in right relationship to Him with what He does for us now that we have been reconciled to Him. What do verses 9 and 10 say is true for those who have been justified by His blood?

8. Through whom are we kept from God's wrath (v. 9)?
    God does not get angry at us when we sin as Christians because He doesn't see our sin! When He looks at us, He sees us as spotless children whose sins have been washed away by the blood of Christ.

Verses 9-11 teach us that if God had compassion for us in our helpless, sinful state before He justified us, then we can be certain that He has compassion on us who have been declared righteous through Christ! He knows we are still helpless apart from Him to do anything that pleases Him.

9. What does verse 11 say is true for those who have been reconciled to God?

Do you find yourself rejoicing? Yes / No
If not, could it be because you do not truly believe that God is holding nothing against you, that even when you are struggling with sin, He still sees you as totally pure—not on the basis of what you are doing, but on the basis of what Christ has done for you?

It is crucial that you understand that when you are sinning, you are still able to approach Him because this is when you need Him the most! The reason we are drawn to sin in the first place is that we have tried to live apart from Him and have not allowed Him to meet the needs of our hearts.

Let's look at what is being compared and contrasted in verses 12-21:

10. Through what man did sin enter the world (v. 12)?

11. Through what man are we justified, or in other words, made righteous (vv. 15-16, 18)?

12. What was the result of the trespass (or sin) of one man (v. 15)?

13. According to Romans 6:23, what was the result of the gift that came by the grace of one man (v. 15)?

14. What did the one man's sin bring, according to verses 16 and 18?

15. What was the result of one act of righteousness according to verses 16 and 18?

16. What came upon all men as a result of Adam's sin (vv. 12, 17)?

17. What came as a result of God's abundant provision of grace for those who receive it (vv. 17-18)?

18. Through whose disobedience were many made sinners (vv. 12, 19)?

19. Through whose obedience will many be made righteous (vv. 17, 19)?

20. Why was the law given (vv. 13, 20)?

21. What was the result of the increase of sin (v. 20)?

22. What reigned before grace became our master (v. 21)?

23. What did it produce (v. 12)?

24. Because of Christ, what reigns over us now (v. 21)?

25. What does it produce (v. 21)?

    J.B. Phillips translates verses 20-21 in *The New Testament in Modern English* as follows:
    Now we find that the Law keeps slipping into the picture to point the vast extent of sin. Yet, though sin is shown to be wide and deep, thank God his grace is wider and deeper still! The whole outlook changes—sin used to be the master of men and in the end handed them over to death: now grace is the ruling factor, with righteousness as its purpose and its end the bringing of men to the eternal life of God through Jesus Christ our Lord.

26. According to the Phillips translation, what purpose does grace have?

Do you see that it is the grace of God that produces righteousness in us?

27. If the grace of God teaches us to live righteous lives (Titus 2:11-14), then when we are struggling with sin, which do we need to better understand: God's standard of righteousness or His grace?

28. Read Colossians 1:6 and then fill in the blank: The gospel had been bearing fruit and growing in the Colossians since the day they heard it and "understood God's grace in all its _____."

    Grace is truth. It does not stand in opposition to truth and, therefore, does not need to be kept "in balance" with truth as some teach. God's grace manifested toward us in our inability to conquer the sins in our lives is the very thing that we need to overcome those sins.

29. Read Hebrews 13:9-10. How does verse 9 say that our hearts are strengthened?

30. Read Titus 3:3-7. What does verse 4 say prompted God to save us?

31. What does Romans 2:4 say leads us to repentance?

What are you allowing to reign over your heart today? Is your goal to be more disciplined to overcome sin, or are you resting in the kindness and love of your Savior who has already won the victory for you? If you are struggling with the burden of sin in your life, rest in His great love for you and trust His grace to set you free.

Week 8
Day 4: John 10:1-30

Read John 10:1-30.

1. In verse 1, to whom do you think Jesus was referring when he talked about the man who does not enter the sheep pen by the gate? (See John 9:40-41.)

2. Verse 9 helps to explain verse 1. Who is the gate of the sheep pen?

3. Had the Pharisees entered the sheep pen by way of the gate? Yes / No

4. Read Luke 18:9. What were the Pharisees trusting in?

5. According to John 10:11, who is the shepherd of the sheep talked about in verse 2?

It is clear that Jesus is both the gate to the sheep pen and the shepherd. Jesus never identifies who the watchman is, yet the primary thing we learn from the mention of the watchman is that he opens for the shepherd because the shepherd has rightful entrance. The shepherd belongs with his sheep.

6. In verses 3-4 what two things do the sheep do?

    1.)
    2.)

7. What does verse 5 say the sheep will never do?

8. Have you heard Christ call your name? I do not mean audibly. Have you heard Him speak to your heart and call you by name? If so, describe how you have heard Him calling.

9. According to verse 9, when Christ leads His sheep out, where does He take them?

10. Read Psalm 23:1-2 and describe the type of pasture that He leads His sheep to.

11. How does it make you feel to know that the pasture where He is leading you is green and restful?

Need you be afraid of following Him?

12. According to John 10:4, how many of His sheep does He lead to find pasture?

13. According to verse 4, why do the sheep follow Him?

14. How do you get to the place where you recognize someone's voice?

15. Read 2 Peter 2:1, 19. What does verse 19 say that false prophets offer to people?

What in reality do they have to offer?

16. According to John 10:4-5, what keeps us from listening to the voices (other than the Shepherd's) that are calling out to us promising freedom, peace, and happiness?

17. A sheep pen was a place of safety for the sheep. The shepherd would lie down in the doorway of the pen (literally becoming a gate) and physically protect the sheep from the dangers outside. If this is true, what type of place do we find ourselves in when we enter through the gate?

18. By whom do we go in and out to find safety and pasture?

19. Verse 10 contrasts the thief to the shepherd. Why does the thief come to the sheep pen?

20. For what two reasons did Jesus come (v. 10)?

21. Verses 11-13 contrast the good shepherd with the hired hand. What does the good shepherd do for the sheep?

Is the hired hand willing to risk his life for the sheep?

22. Why does the hired hand run away when he sees the wolf coming (v. 13)?

23. Read Ezekiel 34:1-15. Who do you think Jesus is referring to in John 10:12-13 when He talks about the hired hand?

24. In John 10:14-15, Jesus said He knows His sheep and His sheep know Him in the same way that the Father knows Him and He knows the Father. What is your response to knowing that Christ compares His relationship with you to His Father's relationship with Him?

25. This is not the only time Jesus compares His relationship with His followers to the Father's relationship with Him. In John 15:9, where Jesus gives a similar analogy, what does Jesus say He has done for His disciples that the Father had done for Him?

26. Jesus describes His relationship with the Father in John 10:30. Read this verse and then read John 17:20-23. What does Jesus pray for His sheep that is true of His relationship with the Father?

27. Read 1 Corinthians 6:15-17. Who do these verses say we, as believers in Christ, are one with?
    When we unite ourselves with Christ, we become one with Him. (Sounds like marriage, doesn't it?) Compare this with John 10:30 where Jesus says that He and the Father are one. Isn't it amazing that we are one with Christ who is one with the Father!

28. Read John 5:19-20. In John 5:20, what two things do we learn about the Father in His relationship to His Son?

    1.)
    2.)

In John 10:15, right after talking about His Father's relationship with Him, Jesus said, "I lay down my life for the sheep." The same love that Jesus knew His Father had for Him, Jesus has for His sheep, and giving His life for them was the full expression of His great love (John 15:13).

Jesus *knows* us in the same way that the Father *knows* His Son, and we can *know* Christ in the same way that He *knows* the Father (John 10:14-15). Jesus *loves* us as much as the Father *loves* His Son (John 15:9). Finally, Christ *is one with* the Father, and we *have become one with* Christ (1 Corinthians 6:15-17). I love the beauty of this intimacy that Jesus wants with us, and the extent to which He went in order to gain it. His sheep know Him and follow Him because they cannot spurn the love of such a passionately loving Savior.

29. Read Ezekiel 34:2-3; Psalm 80:1. The Jews were familiar with these Old Testament passages and quickly would have identified the sheep that Jesus talked about in John 10:1-15 as the people of Israel. Who are the "other sheep" that verse 16 refers to? (See Matthew 28:19, Romans 1:16, Ephesians 2:11-13, and Revelation 7:9-10.)

30. From whom had Jesus received the command to lay down His life and to take it up again (v.18)?

31. According to John 14:31, what motivated Jesus to do exactly what His Father had commanded Him?

32. Read 1 John 3:16-18. Because Jesus laid down His life for us, what are we commanded to do?

33. Will those who are His sheep obey this command (John 10:27)?

34. What three things does Jesus say are true of His sheep in John 10:28?

    1.)
    2.)
    3.)

35. Not only will Jesus not allow His sheep to be snatched from His hand, who else is holding onto and protecting the sheep (v. 29)?
    How does this make you feel?
    Can you rest in your Good Shepherd's and loving Father's hands?

Week 8
Day 5: Psalm 33 and Other Scriptures about God's Merciful, Unfailing Love

Read Psalm 33.

1. To whom are the words of this psalm addressed (v. 1)?

2. According to Romans 1:16-17 and 5:19, who are the righteous?

3. If this is true, why is it appropriate for the upright to praise the Lord?

4. What does verse 5 say that the earth is full of?

5. According to verse 18, in what do those who fear the Lord have their hope?

6. What does the psalmist ask God to cause to rest on His people who put their hope in Him (v. 22)?
    Read these verses in the King James Version (below) and underline the words that are used in place of "unfailing love":

Verse 5: He loveth righteousness and judgment: the earth is full of the goodness of the LORD.
Verse 18: Behold, the eye of the LORD is upon them that fear him, upon them that hope in his mercy;
Verse 22: Let thy mercy, O LORD, be upon us, according as we hope in thee.

The Hebrew word, which the NIV translates as "unfailing love" in the above verses, is used numerous times in the Old Testament to describe God's attitude toward us. Describe what you learn about God's unfailing love (or mercy) from the following scriptures (each one uses this same Hebrew word, shown in italics):

7. Surely goodness and *love* will follow me all the days of my life . . . (Psalm 23:6)

8. Remember not the sins of my youth and my rebellious ways; according to your *love* remember me, for you are good, O Lord. (Psalm 25:7)

9. All the ways of the Lord are *loving* and faithful for those who keep the demands of his covenant. (Psalm 25:10)

10. I will be glad and rejoice in your *love*, for you saw my affliction and knew the anguish of my soul. (Psalm 31:7)

11. Many are the woes of the wicked, but the Lord's *unfailing love* surrounds the man who trusts in Him. (Psalm 32:10)

12. But I am like an olive tree flourishing in the house of God; I trust in God's *unfailing* love for ever and ever. (Psalm 52:8)

13. For great is your *love*, reaching to the heavens; your faithfulness reaches to the skies. (Psalm 57:10)

14. O my Strength, I sing praise to you; you, O God, are my fortress, my *loving* God. (Psalm 59:17)

15. You are forgiving and good, O Lord, abounding in *love* to all who call to you. (Psalm 86:5)

16. Satisfy us in the morning with your *unfailing love*, that we may sing for joy and be glad all our days. (Psalm 90:14)

17. But from everlasting to everlasting the Lord's *love* is with those who fear him . . . (Psalm 103:17)

18. His *love* endures forever. (This is repeated over and over in Psalm 118:1, 2, 3, 4, 29 and in every verse of Psalm 136.)

19. For I desire *mercy*, not sacrifice, and acknowledgment of God rather than burnt offerings. (Hosea 6:6.)

20. He has showed you, O man, what is good. And what does the Lord require of you? To act justly and to love *mercy*, and to walk humbly with your God. (Micah 6:8)

We see from these passages that the same Hebrew word that can be translated into English as "love," or "unfailing love," can also be translated "mercy." The difference between grace and mercy is that grace can be defined as receiving what one does not deserve (see Lesson 7) whereas mercy is *not* receiving what one *does* deserve.

Christ considered it a crucial matter that we understand our need for God's mercy and unfailing love and how God has extended His great mercy and love to us. Read these New Testament passages where He talks about the importance of mercy, and write what you observe:

21. Matthew 9:9-13

22. Matthew 12:1-8

23. Matthew 23:23

Do you see how trusting in God's mercy (or unfailing love) enables us to be merciful, loving people? The Pharisees were unable to show mercy because they did not see God as a merciful God whose love was unfailing. They thought they could earn His favor and thought that those who did not keep the law would be judged.

24. Read James 2:12-13 and fill in the blank:
    "_____ triumphs over judgment!"

25. What does James 2:13 tell us will be shown to those who do not extend mercy to others?

26. Read Titus 3:3-7. What did God extend to us when we were living in rebellion toward Him (v. 5)?

27. Read Ephesians 2:1-9. When we were separated from God by our sin, what prompted Him to raise us to life and seat us with Him in the heavenly realms with Christ (v. 4)?

28. What reason did He have for doing this (v. 7)?

29. Read 1 Peter 1:3. What caused God the Father to give us new birth?

30. Read Psalm 33:18-22 as a prayer of praise to God.

Week 9
Day 2: John 4:1-42

Read John 4:1-42.

1. Why do you suppose Jesus asked the Samaritan woman for a drink (v. 7)?

2. The Samaritan woman was surprised He would ask her for a drink. Why (v. 9)?

3. Jesus replied to her question by saying that if she knew the gift of God, she would be asking Him for a drink. What is the gift of God, according to Romans 5:15-18; 6:23 (compare John 10:10)?

4. What did Jesus say that He would have given her if she had asked Him (v. 10)?

5. John 7:37-39 tells us what He meant by living water. What does John 7:39 say is the living water that flows from within those who believe in Him?

6. What does water do for a physical body?

7. Can you live without it?

8. What did Jesus say that the living water He would give would do for the one who drank it (John 4:13-14)?

9. What did Jesus say that the water He gives becomes (v. 14)?

Just as water gives physical life, so the Spirit gives spiritual life. What does this mean for us, practically speaking?

10. Jesus whetted her desire for water that would forever quench her thirst. What kind of water did she think He was talking about, physical or spiritual (v. 15)?

11. But Jesus knew the woman was really longing for something she had not found. What was she longing for, and where had she been looking to find it (vv. 17-18)?

The woman was longing to be loved but did not realize that only God could give her the love that she craved. She was keen to her physical thirst but failed to see that she had an even greater spiritual thirst. It is easy for us to recognize our physical needs and not even realize that we have even more intense spiritual longings.

12. What are the things your soul most deeply longs for?

As you reflect on your own life today, do you truly feel that your soul is satisfied? Yes / No

13. Read Jeremiah 2:13. Who is the spring (or source) of living water according to Jeremiah 2:13?

14. Instead of drinking from the spring of living water, what did God say His people had done?

15. What "cistern" do you think the Samaritan woman had unwittingly dug to satisfy the needs of her soul?

One of the cisterns I built in my own life was a cistern of selfish ambition, looking to my gifts and abilities to make me feel worth and satisfaction.

16. What cisterns have you built in order to find fulfillment?

17. Have they held water for you (truly satisfied you)?

18. What does Proverbs 19:22 say a person desires?

19. In Psalm 63:1-5 David expressed that it was God who satisfied his longings. What specifically about God caused David to want to glorify and praise Him as long as he lived (vv. 3-4)?

20. Read Psalm 62:5-7. This verse says there is only one place our soul can find rest. Where is it?

21. Where does our hope come from (v. 5)?

22. What three things does verse 6 say that God is for us?

23. What does each of these things mean to you?

24. What two things does verse 7 say depend on God?

25. What two things does verse 7 say that God is for us?

26. Now look back at your list of the things your soul most deeply longs for (question #12) and compare your list to what Psalm 62:5-7 says God is for us. Can you see how He is the one that you are really longing for?

27. Now look back at the Samaritan woman's response to Jesus telling her the details of her life. Read John 4:19. What did she believe must be true about Jesus?

28. Like so many of us, she seemed to think it was exceedingly important to God where people go for worship (v.20). What did Jesus' reply in verses 21-24 reveal was much more important to Him?

Not only do we long for relationship with God, God Himself desires relationship with us! It is not a matter of going to a certain place or performing certain duties that God desires of us, rather He is looking for people whose hearts are truly full of reverence and adoration for Him. He wants our hearts.

29. What do the woman's two comments in verse 25 tell you about her?

30. We know from verse 25 that she was looking for the Messiah. Her words also seem to indicate that she was looking forward to knowing and understanding the truth. How do you suppose she felt when Christ declared, "I who speak to you am he" (v. 26)?

31. What did she leave when she went back to the town (v. 28)?

32. Why do you suppose she left it?

33. What did she say to the people in the town (vv. 28, 39, 41-42)?

The woman realized she had found what her soul had been looking for all along, and when she found Him, it appears she even forgot about her physical need for water because she left her water pot!

34. Is your soul thirsty? Jesus said, "If anyone is thirsty, let him come to me and drink." (John 7:37)

35. How do we drink of Him (John 6:35, 7:38)?

As you close your time in God's Word today, read Isaiah 55:1-3, Revelation 21:6, and Revelation 22:17. Rejoice in what He has given you at no cost and in the everlasting covenant of love that He has made with you (Isaiah 55:3) simply because you have believed in Him.

Week 9
Day 3: Song of Songs 1

Song of Songs was written by King Solomon to describe the love between him and his Shulammite wife. I believe God inspired Solomon to write it not only to portray the beauty and purity of a married couple in love, but also to give us a picture of the relationship between Christ and His bride, the church. The relationship of Christ to the church being compared to earthly marriage is a profound mystery (according to Ephesians 5:32) that we will not totally understand until we see Christ, but we can grasp some understanding of it as we relate it to marriage between a loving husband and wife. As you read portions from the Song of Songs this week, think of the "Lover's" words being Christ's words for you and the "Beloved's" words being your response to His love.

Read Song of Songs 1.

1. Describe how the Beloved feels about her Lover (vv. 2-4).

2. The Beloved saw herself as lovely (v. 5). In 1:15, 2:2, 10, 13, and 14, what does the Lover keep repeating to His Beloved?

3. Read Ephesians 5:25-32. According to verse 27, if you have trusted Christ as your Savior, how does He view you?

4. What did Christ do to make us "radiant" (or "glorious") (Ephesians 5:25-27; Colossians 1:21-22)?

We can go to God with all our blemishes because He does not see them! Christ has washed us and we are pure in His sight.

5. What had made the Beloved's skin dark (Song of Songs 1:5-6)?

6. Working in the sun in the vineyards had made her dark. How have you been "darkened" by the demands people have placed on you?

7. Have people caused you to neglect your own needs (v.6)?

8. Read 1:5 and 2:1. It is interesting that the Beloved saw herself as lovely even though she was dark (which was evidently not considered beautiful at that time). After reading what her Lover kept repeating to her, why do you think she saw herself as beautiful?

9. Do you believe the words of your Lover—that you truly are "without stain or wrinkle or any other blemish, but holy and blameless" (Ephesians 5:27)?

10. Why do you suppose the Beloved wanted to know where her Lover led his sheep to graze and to rest (Song of Songs 1:7)?

11. Your Lover also leads His sheep to graze and to rest (John 10:3-4, 9; Psalm 23:2-3). Do you long to be with Him and join Him in what He is doing?

    The Beloved longed to be with her Lover. When we understand the deep love and acceptance Christ has for us, we long to be near Him and bask in His presence. We also desire to go where He goes and be a part of what He is doing.

12. In verses 9-11 the Lover describes to his Beloved how beautiful she is to him. What does he say he will do for her in verse 11?

13. Read Isaiah 61:10. What has the Lord done for you?

14. What did the Beloved wear for her Lover (v. 12)?

15. What causes us to be fragrant to God (2 Corinthians 2:14-16)?

It is not our good deeds that are fragrant to God, but rather Christ Himself.

Not only does Christ make us look beautiful, but He makes us smell beautiful!

16. What was the Lover like to the Beloved (Song of Songs 1:13-14)?

17. Compare the fragrance of myrrh and henna blossoms to what Christ is to you. What does 2 Corinthians 2:15-16 say that Christ is to us who are being saved?

18. Are you enjoying His fragrance, or are you trying to improve your aroma?

(It is not our goodness that others need, but it is the love of Christ in us and flowing out of us that is truly a fragrance of life to them.)

19. We saw previously that the Lover continually remarked about His Beloved's beauty. In Songs of Songs 1:15-16, what is her response to him when he does so?

20. What do you think prompted her to describe their bed (v. 16)?

21. Read Isaiah 61:3. Who has crowned you with beauty and caused you to display His splendor?

22. When Christ reminds you of the beauty that He now sees in you, what is your response to Him?

23. The Lover was captivated by his Beloved's beauty, and her response in Song of Songs 1:16 was to praise him for his handsome appearance and to want to give herself completely to him. How is your response similar to the Beloved's?

24. The Lover had built a beautiful palace out of cedars and firs for his Beloved (v. 17, 1 Kings 7:1-2, 7-8). What is Jesus doing right now for you (John 14:2-4)?

Week 9
Day 4: Song of Songs 2:1-7

Read Song of Songs 2:1-7.

1. The Beloved knew she was beautiful to her Lover (v. 1). Why do you suppose she spoke of her own beauty?

2. Read Ephesians 5:25-28. What makes us beautiful to Christ?

When we understand that we are beautiful to Christ—not because of anything we have done, but because of what He has made us—we can present ourselves to Him with confidence.

3. What was the Lover's response to His Beloved (v. 2)?

4. Read Mark 15:17-20 and Hebrews 12:2. Who was the joy set before Jesus when He endured the thorns on His head and the suffering on the cross?

Dear sister in Christ, YOU were the lily among the thorns for Jesus that day! When you placed your faith in Him as your Savior, all He experienced on the cross was worth it to Him. Likewise, those who do not trust in Christ for their cleansing and purity are like thorns to Him (Matthew 7:15-16, Hebrews 6:7-9).

5. In verses 3-7 we see how enraptured the Beloved is by her Lover. In verse 3 she compares him to an apple tree and all the other young men to the other trees of the forest. What does this indicate that she found in him that none of the other men could give her?

6. What have you found in Christ that only He can give you?

7. Read 2 Corinthians 11:2-4. What was Paul concerned would lead the Corinthians away from their pure devotion to Christ?

We are led away from Christ when we look to "a different gospel" (to anyone or anything other than Him that promises us fulfillment and satisfaction). The Beloved knew that only her Lover could fulfill her.

8. The Beloved delighted to "sit in her Lover's shade" (v. 3). Read Psalm 91:1 and 121:5-6. How do these verses describe what the Lord is to us?

9. What do you experience when you "sit in [His] shade"?

10. What was sweet to the Beloved's taste (v. 3)?

11. Read Psalm 34:8 and 1 Peter 2:3. If you have "tasted" the Lord, what have you found Him to be like?

When we take refuge in our Lover, He, like the apple tree, nourishes and refreshes us with His goodness and becomes for us a place of rest and protection from the scorching heat of the trials and cares of this world.

12. Where had the Lover taken his Beloved in verse 4?

The Beloved speaks of how her lover took her into his home and set a banquet before her.

13. Where has Christ taken you (Hebrews 10:19-22, Ephesians 2:18, Hebrews 13:10)?

14. Read Psalm 23:5. What does this verse say the Lord has provided for you there?

15. As the Beloved sat at the table, delighting in all the rich foods her lover had provided for her, she was overcome by the love that he lavished on her. Whether literally or figuratively we do not know, but above her head she could see the words: "This is the one that I love." Christ has given us access to His Father by sitting us at His table, and He is continually proclaiming His love for us both to us and to the Father. Read Hebrews 12:22-24. The Greek word for "speaks" in verse 24 is a present active participle, which indicates ongoing action. What is it that continually speaks to God the Father of Christ's love for us and of the purity and beauty we now have?

    The blood of Christ that was shed for us speaks of His tremendous love for us. "Greater love has no one than this, that he lay down his life for his friends" (John 15:13). Christ has made us worthy to sit at His Father's table and to freely commune with Him, all the while His blood testifying of His passionate love for us: "I have loved you with an everlasting love; I have drawn you with loving-kindness" (Jeremiah 31:3).

16. What was the Beloved's response to being loved like this (verse 5)?

17. She was so enraptured by this love that she felt faint! When we are overcome by the love of Christ for us, we are overwhelmed by our weakness and incapability of giving anything back. What did the Beloved ask for to give her strength?

18. If her Lover was to her an apple tree (v. 3), then where would she get the apples to strengthen her?

19. Whose fruit strengthens us in our weakness (Galatians 5:22)?

20. Whose support did she feel in verse 6?

21. Not only was she supported by his left arm, but what was his right arm doing?

22. Read Deuteronomy 33:27 and Psalm 139:10. Whose arms are under you and whose right hand is tightly holding you?

Shutting out all cares in your life and anything that could distract you, take a few moments to close your eyes and mentally picture yourself being supported and held there in His arms, allowing yourself to rest in His love. (Making this a regular practice is helpful in finding refuge in the love of God on an ongoing basis.)

23. Resting in her Lover's arms, the Beloved imposes a request. What does she say to the daughters of Jerusalem (v. 7)?

24. What do you think she means by this?

She doesn't want to be disturbed. She doesn't want anyone to awaken her out of the love that she is experiencing. She wants to rest in her Lover's arms until she has been completely assured of his love and strengthened by his comfort. Will you do the same right now?

Week 9
Day 5: Song of Songs 2:8-16, 4:7-16

Read Song of Songs 2:8-16.

1. Whose voice did the Beloved hear (v. 8, 10)?

2. Whose voice calls to you (John 10:3)?

3. Why do you suppose the Lover was running so fast (Song of Songs 2:8-9)?

4. Read Luke 15:20 and 19:10. Who runs toward you?

5. What did the Lover call his Beloved (Song of Songs 2:10, 13)?

6. What does your Lover call you (Colossians 3:12)?

7. What did the Lover tell his Beloved to do in verses 10 and 13?

8. Why do you suppose he had to say it twice?

9. Have you heard Christ speaking this to your heart (John 10:3-4, 9)?

10. What two things did he point out that were now in her past (Song of Songs 2:11)?

11. What season had arrived (vv. 12-13)?

12. What does 2 Corinthians 5:17 say is now in your past?

13. What does it say has now come?

14. Christ wants to be with you and for you to enjoy His presence and relish the new life He has given you. Will you respond to His bidding?

15. What does the Lover call His Beloved in Song of Songs 2:14?

16. Doves mate for life. What significance do you think this fact may have had in the name that he gave her?

17. Where was the Beloved in verse 14?

18. The Lover did not want her to be hidden from him. What did he want to see (v. 14)?

19. Why did he want to see her face (v. 14)?

20. Christ wants your face turned toward Him. Why do we not have to hide ourselves from His holy presence (Hebrews 9:14, 4:16)?

Imagine the joy that it brings to Christ's heart to see our faces turned toward Him in confidence because He has made us pure and spotless with no wrinkle or blemish!

21. What is the Lover longing to hear (Song of Songs 2:14)?

22. What does her voice sound like to him (v. 14)?

23. Does your Lover want to hear your voice (1 Thessalonians 5:17)?

24. How does your Lover feel about hearing the voice of His redeemed Beloved (Proverbs 15:8)?

25. What do you suppose the Lover meant when he said, "Catch for us the foxes, the little foxes that ruin the vineyards" (Song of Songs 2:15)?

26. The Lover had called her to come with him and enjoy the blossoming vines (v. 13), but little foxes would come and destroy the vines. Jesus called Himself the vine and us the branches and said we can only bear fruit as we remain in Him. With this in mind, what are the little foxes that keep you from resting in Him and producing fruit?

27. What does Hebrews 12:1 tell us to do with these hindrances?

28. What is the Beloved's response to her Lover's pursuit of her and desire to experience life with her (v.16)? She said, "My lover is _____, and I am _____."

What did Jesus call the sheep that He (the Good Shepherd) brings out in John 10:4? He said, "When he has brought out all _____ _____, he goes on ahead of them, and his sheep follow him because they know his voice."

Jesus tenderly calls you His own. Do you call Him yours?

29. How does the Lover describe his bride in Song of Songs 4:7?

30. Do you long to be seen this way?

31. Dear sister in Christ, you are seen this way! What has Christ done to make you flawless (Colossians 1:22, Ephesians 5:27)?

32. What does the Lover want His bride to do (v. 8)?
    He longs to be with her! Why (v. 9)?

33. What did it take for her to have his heart (v. 9)?
    All we have to do is to look at Jesus and we have His heart (Numbers 21:8-9, John 3:14-18). We don't have to clean ourselves up—He does that for us, and dresses us with His righteousness as a bride adorns herself with jewels (Isaiah 61:10). He takes great joy in the beauty that is ours simply because we have trusted in Him to give it to us.

34. In Song of Songs 4:10, what does the Lover talk about that brings him great delight?
    Read Isaiah 62:5. Do you believe that God rejoices over you in the same way that a bridegroom rejoices over his bride?

35. In Song of Songs 4:11, what does the Lover say drips from his bride's lips?
    What does he say is under her tongue?
    What do Psalm 19:9-10 and Psalm 119:103 compare to honey?
    First Peter 2:2 (JKV) says, "As newborn babes, desire the sincere milk of the word, that ye may grow thereby."
    With these verses in mind, what "milk" and "honey" drip from you, according to John 15:3 and Ephesians 5:26? Can we take the credit for our "sweetness"?
    In Song of Songs 4:10. 11, the Lover also talks about how much he enjoys his Beloved's fragrance. As we learned from 2 Corinthians 2:14-16, Christ is the one responsible for our sweet fragrance. This reminds me of the expensive perfume my husband gave me for our anniversary. He gave it to me so that I would wear it when I was near him. Christ, too, lavishes us with His own perfume so that we will come near Him and allow Him to enjoy our sweet aroma.

36. In Song of Songs 4:12, the Lover compares his Beloved to a garden and a spring (indicating her beauty and the satisfaction that she gives him). What adjectives does he use to describe the garden and spring?

37. In Proverbs 5:15-20, Solomon (who also wrote Song of Songs) uses the metaphors of a cistern, well, and fountain to describe a wife whose "water" is to be for her husband alone. With this in mind, why do you think Solomon uses the adjectives *locked up* and *sealed* to describe his bride in Song of Songs 4:12?

38. The Beloved's love was for her Lover alone. What had he alone enjoyed from his "garden" (vv. 13-14)?

39. What had he alone enjoyed from his "fountain" and "well" (v. 15)?

40. The Lover enjoyed the fruit, spices, and fragrances he received from his garden. When we bask in the love of our Savior, what fruit and aroma do we give out for Him to enjoy (John 15:4-5, 8-9; Galatians 5:22; 2 Corinthians 2:14-16)?

    Who is the one actually producing the fruit in us and the aroma that He delights in?

    Our Lover is jealous to have all of our love and devotion but knows that we are helpless to give Him any love or affection at all unless we receive His love for us (1 John 4:19). As we go to Him to be loved, His love fills us up and overflows into a fountain of love directed toward Him and Him alone as the only true Lover of our souls (John 7:38). When we understand His great love for us, we desire to give our heart's devotion to no other Lover but Him.

41. What is the Beloved's response to her Lover's comparison of her to a garden (v. 16)?

42. Who does she want to come into the garden to enjoy its fruits (v. 16)?

    Oh, Spirit of Christ, breathe on us that Your fragrance and beauty would emanate from us! Jesus, thank you that Your desire is for us, that we have captivated You with a mere glance in Your direction. We are overwhelmed by such love. May we give our love to You and You alone. "Should [our] springs overflow in the streets, [our] streams of water in the public squares? Let them be yours alone, never to be shared with strangers" (Proverbs 5:16-17).

Leader's Guide

Introductory Session

In your first group meeting, concentrate on getting acquainted with one another, helping group members become familiar with the format and contents of the study. Here are some suggestions:

1. Have members introduce themselves and share what they hope to get out of the study.

2. Watch the introductory video.

3. Make sure everyone has a copy of *Loved: Learning to Rest*.

4. Talk through the different aspects of the study: the nine lessons, the Suggested Daily Schedules," the viewer guides, and the "Going Deeper" exercises. Explain the minimum expectation: that each member complete one lesson per week ("Going Deeper" is optional).

    You may want to encourage members to do the "Going Deeper" exercises by explaining the benefits of in-depth study of God's Word.

5. Ask those who do the "Going Deeper" homework to underline anything that impacts them as they go through it so that they can be prepared to share it with the group.

6. Talk about the importance of confidentiality so that everyone has the freedom to share honestly. Encourage members to keep what is said strictly within the group.

7. Pray together that God will work in each woman's life in her particular area of need. Encourage the members to commit to pray for one another throughout the next nine weeks.

    Consider dividing the group into prayer partners so that every person is covered in prayer as she completes this study.

8. Collect and share contact information for your group.

Session 1
Questions to Prompt Group Discussion

Greet and welcome members, and pray together. Begin with either the video or inviting the members to briefly share some about the week's lesson or what they learned from the "Going Deeper" scriptures. The discussion questions that follow are for the purpose of reviewing the week's lesson. Discuss these after viewing of the video to ensure that the discussion does not run overtime. These questions are merely a guide. Allow the Spirit of God to lead you with the discussion and to keep the group from straying off topic.

1. Can you relate to Paul's struggle with sin in Romans 7? What did Paul say in this passage that describes your own struggle with sin (p. 4)?

2. Read 2 Corinthians 12:7-9. What does verse 9 teach us about weakness (p. 5)?

3. How has accepting your weakness made a difference in your life?

4. Lesson 1 talked about surrendering to God and making Him the only master that we serve. Clara told how she was trying to serve two masters by trying to please God and people and how she came to realize that it was people she was serving and not God at all (p. 6). When you began this study, did you find yourself trying to serve two masters? If so, whom or what were you serving?

5. If you have the freedom, share some of "the lines" that your sinful nature gives you to keep you from doing what is right (p. 7).

6. Did writing down these "lines" reveal anything to you about the roots of the sin that you deal with (pp. 7-9)? If so, what did you learn from this exercise?

7. What keeps a person from being able to surrender completely to God (p. 9)?

8. Let's say our memory verses together.

   Taste and see that the LORD is good;
       blessed is the man who takes refuge in him.
   Fear the LORD, you his saints,
       for those who fear him lack nothing. (Psalm 34:8-9)

9. Let's pray together, asking God to teach us how good He is so that we might surrender our lives in complete trust to Him.

Session 2
Questions to Prompt Group Discussion

NOTE: Some answers, set in italics, are provided in order to help the group leader guide the discussion.

Greet and welcome members. Pray together.

1. Lesson 2 talked about having our minds set on what the Spirit desires. Share any examples of how the Spirit of God has changed your sinful desires into desires to do His will.

2. Romans 8:5 says, "Those who live according to the sinful nature have their minds set on what that nature desires; but those who live in accordance with the Spirit have their minds set on what the Spirit desires." What does this verse teach us to do in order to have our minds set on what the Spirit desires?

   We simply need to live in accordance with the Spirit (be filled and controlled by Him).

3. How did Clara have Romans 8:5 backwards when she was trying to set her mind on what the Spirit desired (p. 16)?

   Romans 8:5 says that "those who live in accordance with the Spirit have their minds set on what the Spirit desires." It does not say that we need to set our minds on what the Spirit desires in order to live in accordance with the Spirit. Living in accordance with the Spirit actually causes our minds to be set on what the Spirit desires. This is an important difference because we do not have the power to change our mind to want what the Spirit wants. That is the Spirit's job.

4. By trying to set her mind on what the Spirit desired, Clara did begin to experience victory over sin. What reason did she give for this (p. 16)?

   She realized it was not because she had discovered a formula that worked, but because she was beginning to trust God enough to surrender every thought "to make it obedient to Christ" (2 Corinthians 10:5).

5. Clara once believed that the key to victory over sin was simply surrender but discovered there was a deeper reason for not having victory over sin. What did she begin to realize the deeper issue was (p. 17)?

   The deeper issue was trust because we cannot surrender ourselves in obedience to someone we cannot trust.

6. With this in mind, what is the purpose of taking "captive every thought to make it obedient to Christ" (2 Corinthians 10:5) (p. 18)?

   The goal in taking every thought captive is the knowledge of God (knowing who He is). When we reject the wrong thoughts about who God is and replace them with the truth of who He is, we find that we can trust Him and gladly offer the parts of our bodies as instruments of righteousness to Him.

7. This lesson talked about the need to pursue God rather than focusing on getting victory over sin (p. 18). When you began this study, what was your primary focus? Were you intent on getting victory over sin or growing in your knowledge of Christ?

8. Are you beginning to see a difference in your life as you focus on getting to know Christ? If so, how?

9. What did Paul say in Philippians 3:7-14 that he wanted more than anything else (p. 19)?

10. What is the desire of the Lover of our souls according to Song of Songs 7:10 (p. 19)?

    His desire is for us and for our unadulterated love.

11. Let's say our memory verses together.

    For what the law was powerless to do in that it was weakened by the sinful nature, God did by sending his own Son in the likeness of sinful man to be a sin offering. And so he condemned sin in sinful man, in order that the righteous requirements of the law might be fully met in us, who do not live according to the sinful nature but according to the Spirit. (Romans 8:3-4)

12. Let's pray together, asking God to teach us who He is so that we might be filled with Him and the knowledge of what He has done for us and live in glad surrender to His Spirit.

Session 3
Questions to Prompt Group Discussion

Greet and welcome members. Pray together.

1. In lesson 3, Clara explained her struggle with insecurity and pride. Could you relate to this struggle? If so, how did you relate?

2. In what ways has God used your weakness in order to show His power through your life (p. 29)?

3. Have you tried to bear fruit apart from remaining in the Vine? What has this looked like in your life?

4. According to John 15:9, how much does Christ love us (p. 32)?

   Christ loves us as much as the Father loves Christ. Both God the Father's love and Christ's love are perfect, and consequently, Christ loves us every bit as much as the Father loves Him. Perfect love cannot be improved upon.

5. What does it mean to remain in Christ's love (p. 33)?

   It means to live trusting that He loves you, to live mindful of His love, allowing yourself to be wrapped in His loving arms and receiving His love.

6. Why must we know God before we are able to love others (p. 33)?

7. Clara shared about her confrontation through prayer with the stronghold of selfish ambition. What broke the stronghold that night was the truth that God was compassionate toward her (p. 34). If God has met the needs of your heart with His kindness and compassion, how has He revealed His love to you?

8. Let's say our memory verses together.

    Remain in me, and I will remain in you. No branch can bear fruit by itself; it must remain in the vine. Neither can you bear fruit unless you remain in me. I am the vine; you are the branches. If a man remains in me and I in him, he will bear much fruit; apart from me you can do nothing. (John 15:4-5)

9. Let's pray together, asking God to reveal His kindness and compassion to us and keep us abiding in His love.

Session 4
Questions to Prompt Group Discussion

Greet and welcome members. Pray together.

1. When we have no power to overcome strongholds of sin, what must we believe in (p. 39)?

2. It is not enough to believe that Christ has the power to change us. What did Clara find automatically transformed her (p. 40)?

3. Clara keeps reminding us that you cannot trust someone you do not know. According to Romans 10:17, how do you get to know and trust God (p. 41)?

4. In John 8:32, how did Jesus say you can be set free from sin (p. 42)?

5. Second Thessalonians 2:13 says that we are saved through two things. What are they (p. 43)?

6. Psalm 33:18-19 tells us that God comes to the rescue of those who fear Him and whose hope is in what (p. 43)?

7. Describe the life of one who relies on a list of do's and don'ts to please God.

8. Describe how knowing Christ and trusting in how He feels about you is transforming your life.

9. Let's say our memory verses together.

    For we do not have a high priest who is unable to sympathize with our weaknesses, but we have one who has been tempted in every way, just as we are—yet was without sin. Let us then approach the throne of grace with confidence, so that we may receive mercy and find grace to help us in our time of need. (Hebrews 4:15-16)

10. Let's pray together, thanking God for His patience, kindness, and compassion toward us and for making it possible for us to boldly approach His throne of grace.

Session 5
Questions to Prompt Group Discussion

Greet and welcome members. Pray together.

1. What are some of the lies you have believed and what truths from God's Word are you meditating on to renew your mind?

2. How is meditating on truth transforming you?

3. After reminding yourself of truth when the lies come to your mind, what difference are you seeing in your actions?

4. How is knowing the truth about God and the truth about yourself setting you free?

5. Are you experiencing the fruit of the Spirit? If so, how is it being produced in your life?

6. This week, say the verse you chose to memorize to your prayer partner and pray together with her that the power of God's Word will continue to set you free from the lies that have bound you.

Session 6
Questions to Prompt Group Discussion

Greet and welcome members. Pray together.

1. Could you relate to the problem Clara had of feeling the need to make herself presentable to God? If so, how has this struggle manifested itself in your life?

2. Through the sacrifice of Christ's body, what have we been made (p. 64)?

3. What did Christ do after he offered himself as a sacrifice for sins (p. 64)?

   He sat down, signifying that His work was finished. This means there is nothing left for you to do to make yourself acceptable to God. Christ has already accomplished that for you.

4. Do you really believe that God, because of what Christ has done, sees you as a holy, radiant bride without stain or wrinkle or any other blemish? If so, how does the way you live show that you believe this?

5. How has viewing yourself the way God views you changed you from the way you viewed yourself in the past?

6. Why does Satan want us to think we have to get our act together before God will allow us in His presence (p. 65)?

   He knows that by making us feel undeserving of going to God, he can keep us from going to the only One who can help us.

7. Read Romans 8:8. Why is it a true statement to say that we cannot please God by overcoming sin (pp. 65-66)?

   God is not pleased with us for overcoming sin because He knows it is impossible for us to do so. He is the one who has overcome sin in our lives by His finished work on the cross.

8. Read Hebrews 11:5-6. What is the only way we can please God (p. 66)?

9. If we are not to focus on doing the right things to please God, what are we supposed to focus on? (Hebrews 11:6; 12:2)

   The Lord tells us to fix our eyes on Jesus, the author and finisher of our faith, and as we grow in our knowledge of Him, we grow in our faith.

10. Let's say our memory verses together.

    Therefore, there is now no condemnation for those who are in Christ Jesus, because through Christ Jesus the law of the Spirit of life set me free from the law of sin and death. (Romans 8:1-2)

11. Let's pray together, thanking Christ for taking all our sin and shame upon Himself and for making us pure and without blemish in God's sight and free from all condemnation.

Session 7
Questions to Prompt Group Discussion

Greet and welcome members. Pray together.

1. On pages 71-72 is a list of evidences of trusting in self rather than in Christ for daily salvation from sin. Which of these could you relate to and how?

2. What is the key to being saved from sinning on a daily basis? How are we to live the Christian life according to Colossians 2:6-7 (pp. 72-73)?

    In the same way we received Christ Jesus at the point of salvation, we are to live the Christian life: depending completely on Him to save us from sin, being strengthened by Him in faith, and overflowing with thankfulness. The Christian life is about Him and His power to save us, not about our trying through human effort to be like Him.

3. How does it make you feel to realize that "Christ is the end of our struggle for righteousness" (p. 73)?

4. What difference has the realization of this truth made in your life?

5. What is the purpose of confessing our sins to God (p. 76)?

    The purpose of confession is to stop sin or to cause us to turn from our sin; confession is not our way of making up for it.

6. Could you relate to Clara's struggle of feeling the need to go through the ritual of confession in order to feel forgiven? In what way(s) could you relate to it?

7. What do you feel you have to do to be acceptable to God?

8. Has the realization that all your sins are completely forgiven (past, present, and future according to Hebrews and to Colossians 2:13-14) changed you in any way? How has it changed you?

9. When you sin, are you learning to go to Christ to meet the deeper need of your heart that drove you to sin?

10. What do you believe Chafer meant by his words: "God has expressed His love to those He saves by the gracious thing He has done. Christian service for God should be equally gracious" (p. 77)?

    God gave us His love freely and without cost. In the same way, we should serve God freely, without expecting payment. When we serve God with the motive of receiving His acceptance or favor in return, we are not serving Him graciously, but we are serving Him legalistically. Understanding God's grace is vital to serving God in freedom.

11. What did Clara mean when she said that grace and truth are not contradictions that need to be in balance?

    Grace is truth. It is the truth that sets us free from sin.

12. Let's say our memory verses together.

    For the grace of God that brings salvation has appeared to all men. It teaches us to say "No" to ungodliness and worldly passions, and to live self-controlled, upright and godly lives in this present age, while we wait for the blessed hope—the glorious appearing of our great God and Savior, Jesus Christ, who gave himself for us to redeem us from all wickedness and to purify for himself a people that are his very own, eager to do what is good. (Titus 2:11-14)

13. Let's pray together, thanking God for His power to save us, not only from eternal hell, but also from ourselves and our sin on a daily basis.

Session 8
Questions to Prompt Group Discussion

Greet and welcome members. Pray together.

1. As you read the story of Mephibosheth, could you relate to him in any way? If so, in what way (p. 87)?

2. Read Ephesians 1:2-6. Mephibosheth expected to die because he was Saul's grandson, but instead he was given a place at David's table and ate there "like one of the king's sons" (2 Samuel 9:11). Describe what we have been given by Christ, also through no merit of our own (p. 88).

3. Read John 10:28-29. Mephibosheth lived in safety in Jerusalem. As a child of God, where is your place of safety?

4. Before you began this study, how did you view God? Could you relate to Him as to a loving father, or did he seem more like a judge?

5. Has this study changed your view of God? In what ways has your view of Him changed?

6. Read Romans 5:1-2. How have we been justified (p. 88)?

How is it that we have peace with God (p. 89)?

7. In Romans 5:1, the phrase "peace with God" literally means "peace facing God." How would you describe the way you usually feel when you "face God" in prayer (p. 89)?

8. The phrase "the grace in which we now stand" (v. 2) literally means that we are now completely wrapped in cords of grace. A similar picture is presented in Psalm 32:10. What does Psalm 32:10 say surrounds the man who trusts in the Lord (p. 89)?

9. Have you been picturing yourself in Christ's arms with His big robe of righteousness wrapped around you? If so, has this made any difference in the way you live your life?

10. Let's say our memory verses together.

Who will bring any charge against those whom God has chosen? It is God who justifies. Who is he that condemns? Christ Jesus, who died—more than that, who was raised to life—is at the right hand of God and is also interceding for us. (Romans 8:33-34)

11. Let's pray together, thanking God for being an exceedingly gracious, loving Father who has wrapped us up in the righteousness of Christ and brought us close to Himself. He will not allow anyone or anything to separate us from His love.

Session 9
Questions to Prompt Group Discussion

Greet and welcome members. Pray together.

1. What did Clara find helped her in battling her attractions to a man other than her husband?

   She had been learning to let the longings of her soul that once drove her to sin, drive her to her Savior who filled all those longings completely.

2. Has the knowledge that our attraction to sin is the result of looking in the wrong place to get our legitimate needs satisfied helped you in dealing with sin? If so, how?

3. Jeremiah 2:13 says, "My people have committed two sins: They have forsaken me, the spring of living water, and have dug their own cisterns, broken cisterns that cannot hold water."
   In this scripture, the "broken cisterns" represent the things we look to other than God to find fulfillment and satisfaction. They cannot hold water because they were not meant to bring lasting fulfillment and satisfaction. The only spring of living water that can truly satisfy our thirsty souls is God Himself. What cisterns have you dug that have proven unreliable?

4. Describe what you are doing to replace those cisterns with the fountain of living water.

5. Lesson 9 explains that putting on the armor of God is really the same as putting on Christ. Does this understanding help you know how to be spiritually armed? If so, how does it help?

   For Clara, it took the focus off doing something and put it on resting in Christ to fight for her.

6. What does it mean to you to rest in Christ?

7. Read Hebrews 4:1. In this verse, what is meant by "entering his rest"?

   The "rest" that is being talked about here is what we experience when we simply trust in the finished work of Christ to do for us what we could never do for ourselves. The work of salvation was completely accomplished for us by Christ's death and resurrection. Trusting in Him and His character causes us to stop striving to save ourselves from sinning. Human effort can never make us righteous in God's sight.

8. Instead of focusing on either how good we are or how bad we are, to where should we divert our attention (p. 100)?

9. What has been the most life-changing truth that you have learned by doing this study?

10. Let's say our memory verse together.

    The Lord appeared to us in the past, saying: "I have loved you with an everlasting love; I have drawn you with loving-kindness." (Jeremiah 31:3)

11. Let's pray together, thanking God for His everlasting love that is to us a fountain that never runs dry, flowing into and satisfying each and every longing in all the deep crevices of our hearts.

Notes

1. James Strong, *Strong's Exhaustive Concordance*: *Greek Dictionary of the New Testament* (Grand Rapids, Michigan, reprinted 1982), page 47.

2. Jerry Bridges, *Transforming Grace* (Colorado Springs, Colorado: NavPress, 1991), page 112.

3. Lewis Sperry Chafer, D.D., *Grace* (Chicago, Illinois: Moody Press, 1945), page 222.

4. Ibid., page 7.

5. Song of Songs 2:14

6. Song of Songs 2:10-13

7. Song of Songs 1:4

8. Song of Songs 1:2

9. Song of Songs 8:14

10. Song of Songs 8:6-7

11. Song of Songs 7:10

12. James Strong, *Strong's Exhaustive Concordance*: *Greek Dictionary of the New Testament* (Grand Rapids, Michigan, reprinted 1982), page 18.

13. *Complete Commentary on the Whole Bible*, by Matthew Henry, at http://www.sacred-texts.com/bib/cmt/mhcc/luk014.htm, accessed November 24, 2015.

14. The Alliance, *Tozer Devotional*, "To Know Him is to Love Him," http://www.cmalliance.org/devotions/tozer?id=669, accessed November 13, 2015.

15. Warren W. Wiersbe, *The Bible Exposition Commentary, Volume 1* (Wheaton, Illinois: SP Publications, Inc., 1989), page 357.

16. C. I. Scofield, D.D., *The New Scofield Study Bible (NIV)* (New York, New York: Oxford University Press, Inc., 1998), page 692.

17. James Strong, *Strong's Exhaustive Concordance*: *Greek Dictionary of the New Testament* (Grand Rapids, Michigan, reprinted 1982), page 23.

18. Ibid., page 36.

Made in the USA
San Bernardino, CA
07 February 2016